To millions she was a symbol of sex.

To a handful of men she was but a dollar sign.

To her own mother she was a stepping stone to power.

Sex Goddess, Blonde Bombshell, Golden Girl
—the outlandish vamp in "Red Dust" and "Hell's Angels"
—still others will remember her brilliant
comedic talent in *Dinner At Eight*
and to some, she was just that blonde in the
gold lamé dress who never wore a brassiere.

This is the strange enigma of Jean Harlow.

A story stranger than fiction.

A beautiful young woman with a
very special way of walking,
talking and feeling.

Harlow had it all.
And there hasn't been anyone since.
And perhaps there may never be.

THE
JEAN HARLOW
STORY

Fully Illustrated

by John Pascal

POPULAR LIBRARY · NEW YORK

Front cover photo: PENGUIN PHOTO
Back cover photo: CULVER PICTURES

THE
JEAN HARLOW
STORY

Chapter One

Fusty old historians will tell you that the first atomic bomb was dropped during World War II, but something close to 70 million other people will smile and shake their heads and say the historians are wrong. The 70 million, who were there and ought to know, can testify that the first superbomb exploded onto the landscape in 1930, and today, three decades later, the atmosphere is still a little shiny from its radiation.

It detonated across the nation in a motion picture called *Hell's Angels*. The moment of impact came when a soft voice said huskily, "Excuse me while I change into something more comfortable."

What came through the doorway up on

the silver screen a moment or two later was sheathed in the flimsiest of negligees—a stunning, provocative, sexy creature who has come to be known to history as the "Blonde Bombshell."

The bombshell, of course, wasn't an "it." It was a she.

Her name was Jean Harlow, and there has been no one quite like her before or since.

In a blazing career that lasted eight brief years and ended tragically with her death from a complicated illness at the age of twenty-six, Jean Harlow reigned as the unrivaled, unchallenged movie queen of her generation, the bright golden girl of the '30's.

She was the Marilyn Monroe—and more— of her day, a dazzling beauty with wavy flowing platinum blonde hair and, as Clark Gable described it, "the greatest shape, bar none, of any dame I've ever seen."

On the marquee her name was magic, a guaranteed box-office draw that brought capacity audiences to every picture she ever starred in and sent the total gross on her films above the $100 million mark—and they were depression dollars, worth the full 100 cents.

On the screen, she was every man's dream, every woman's vaguely envied ideal, with her

8

great good looks, vivacious figure and what in time became her trademark, the platinum hair.

In some ways, she changed the looks of the American woman. Until Harlow, the vogue was to be flat-chested. Harlow, with her wickedly sexy curves and open décolletage, soon changed that, and the effects are still with us. So, too, with her hair. "Peroxide blondes" were rare in the pre-Harlow days; an oddity, and somehow bizarre. Then Harlow hit the screen and drugstores everywhere in the country were reporting gigantic increases in "bottled blonde."

She was universally adored by men, not only the millions in the audience in every town and hamlet in the nation, but the people she worked with too—the actors, the directors, the producers, even the cameramen, mechanics and electricians. She was "one of the boys," a sprightly, wise-cracking, good-natured buddy to everyone on the set. Tommy Watts, an electrician who worked with her on the set of *Suzy*, one of Jean's later movies, tells of a crap game he and some of the other workers were having one day.

"I was rolling and threw a deuce down," he recalled, "and the next thing I hear is this lady's voice behind me saying, 'You're faded.'

The Jean Harlow Story

I spun around and sure enough, it's Harlow. She won, grabbed the dice, and made three straight passes. Won about ten bucks. Then she walked off laughing."

She was one of the first screen comediennes and she originated a style that's been copied a thousand times over ever since. She brought to a succession of roles a comical characterization of the practical, quick-tongued gold digger with a talent for separating diamonds and apartments from impressionable playboys and sentimental gangsters. All her pictures had overtones of amusingly self-conscious allure. But she could play a magnificent shrike, too, and moviegoers became familiar with her indignant flouncing about and her habit of striding around wildly in her rages.

Everything about Jean Harlow spoke of vivaciousness and good fun. Her effervescent screen personality shone through in *Hell's Angels*, *Suzy*, *Goldie*, *Bombshell*, *Riffraff*, and dozens of others. And yet her private life was marked by tragedy. Two of her three marriages ended in divorce and the other ended when her husband, producer Paul Bern, committed suicide.

And there was, of course, the final tragedy, the uremic poisoning that had begun as influ-

10

enza, grew worse, and ultimately became fatal, killing her at 11:35 A.M., June 7, 1937.

The news shocked the nation and plunged Hollywood into deep grief. The hardest hit of all was William Powell, the distinguished actor with whom Jean Harlow had fallen deeply in love—the only true love in her life. They were almost certain to be married once Powell's divorce was complete. His grief was inconsolable.

Hollywood's attitude was summed up by Louis B. Mayer. "This is the end of a rich personal friendship," he said. "This girl, whom so many millions adored, was one of the loveliest, sweetest persons I have ever known in thirty years of the theatrical business. I have lost a friend, the world has lost a ray of sunlight."

In a way, Jean Harlow's life was a paradox. She had everything anyone could hope for —beauty, fame, wealth, the adoration of men everywhere. And yet happiness—true happiness—eluded her nearly all her life. Only at the end did she find it with William Powell, but death denied her its bright fulfillment.

Twenty-six is a cruelly young age at which to die, but Jean Harlow crowded a lot into her brief time on earth. And the story of Jean

Harlow should not be a story of death, but of life.

For the beginning of that story, it's necessary to go back, back to the very heart of the land she loved and conquered.

Chapter Two

The girl who was to become Jean Harlow was born in Kansas City, Missouri, on March 3, 1911, the daughter of Dr. Montclair Carpenter and his wife Jean. They named her Harlean Carpenter. From the first, Harlean was blessed with strikingly beautiful hair, blonde shading into silver. Everyone says babies are beautiful, but in the case of little Harlean it was an undisputable fact.

Like the tempestuous woman she would become later in Hollywood, Harlean was by turn mischievous, serious, and flippant, capable of remarkable outbursts of fury for a child, but at the same time warmly affectionate, especially toward her mother. Harlean and Jean were closer even than most mothers and daughters—partly because Harlean was an only child, and partly because, as she grew older, trouble came between Dr. and Mrs. Carpenter.

But in the first few years of her life, Harlean's world was serene and happy, darkened only by the fact that at school the other children teased her about her hair.

"Cotton top," the girls would chant at her, "Cotton top. Harlean is a cotton top!"

Harlean would run home in tears to her mother, screaming at her tormentors. "I hate them!" A torrent of tears would moisten her cheeks. "I hate them all!"

"Now, now," Mrs. Carpenter would say, as Harlean buried her tear-stained face in Mother's lap, "they're only jealous. They only wish *they* had such beautiful hair."

"Really?" Harlean would ask hopefully.

"Of course, punkin. Your hair is your crowning glory."

"Well. . . ." Harlean replied doubtfully.

"Come, Harlean. Look in the mirror."

Mrs. Carpenter held up a hand mirror for her sprightly daughter, and, as the girl gazed upon herself critically, she assured her that, "as long as they tease you and run after you, just remember: they're jealous and wish they could be as beautiful."

Harlean nodded her head abruptly. "All right, Mother. But I *still* hate them!" And she bounced from the room.

During these early quiet, uneventful years, Harlean spent lazy summers out on the Kansas flatlands with her grandmother, Mrs. S. D. Harlow, her mother's mother. Her mother's maiden name, as can now be seen, was Jean Harlow. Such was the closeness between them that, when fame beckoned, Harlean adopted her mother's name.

But all that was far away during the World War I years of 1915, 1916, 1917, and 1918 when Harlean spent her girlhood near Bonner Springs, Kansas. There was no hint, then, that a famous movie about that war would launch Jean Harlow into international acclaim.

In Mrs. Harlow's sprawling home near Bonner Springs, a home called "Red Gables," little Harlean was known as "Baby." Home was Grandma Harlow, and the great Kaw River that flowed past Red Gables.

"She spent several childhood summers with us," Mrs. Harlow would remember later. "There is where I grew to know what kind of a child my granddaughter was. It's the picture I like best to remember of her, a picture that

15

many people who saw her only as a hussy or a vamp in movie roles would hardly believe. I can understand her. She was really a serious girl at heart, and a good girl. Imaginative and impulsive; full of life, too."

Mrs. Harlow remembered, too, an incident which showed the sentimental and affectionate side of little Harlean. "I remember she came to our home one day—she was only seven—and handed me her baby ring and bracelet she had outgrown."

"You keep them for me, Grandmother," Harlean said. "I don't ever want to lose them or forget them."

In later years, Jean took great delight in recounting the details of her childhood. She once told an interviewer: "I was born in a marvelous old gray stone house on Olive Street in Kansas City. The house belonged to my grandparents and my mother and father were living there at the time. Mother tells me now that I created an immediate though joyous problem. It seems that they had all fully expected me to be a boy and were prepared with a perfect boy's name. Since my family's name was Carpenter and my mother's maiden name was Harlow, the child's name was to be Harlow Carpenter. A compromise was

16

quickly reached and they had me christened Harlean, the nearest feminine name the family could invent to resemble Harlow.

"Dad was a doctor, and his father a prosperous real estate broker. Mother was an only child and very attached to her family. My grandparents were so delighted with the idea of a tow-headed little tot livening up the old gray stone house again that they insisted we all remain together. So, for the first two years of my life, I was the little princess catered to by four loving adults. I'm sure my grandparents were the most doting relatives a child could ever have. As a result I became a small, pampered tyrant who, at two years old, was in complete control of the house.

"My grandfather was the worst. During the day, when he should have been in his office, he would sneak home to play with me—and give my mother and grandmother absurd excuses for playing hooky from his office. All through my childhood, Grandfather and I were boon companions. I believe he had more influence in molding my thoughts and ideas than any other person.

"When I was two, Mother and Dad decided that they were ready for a home of their own, and Mother was beginning to worry about the effect all the pampering and attention would have on me. She had her own ideas about raising children—that if they were petted and humored too often they might become very disagreeable and unmanagable. A family conference was called, everyone agreed, and, a few days after my birthday, we moved to the new house overlooking one of Kansas City's most beautiful parks.

"Summers, though, were laughed away at Grandfather's house. I remember it so well, big and rambling with cool rooms and seven gables that peeked out from beneath a red roof. It was built high upon a bluff overlooking the Missouri River and we called it 'Red Gables.' We had wonderful summers, picnicking beneath the mighty, gnarled, spreading trees, taking boat rides on the river, hiking and horseback riding. Horseback riding was my favorite, and Grandfather bought me a little Shetland pony I called "Babe." Babe had a silver-mounted saddle bridle, and the saddest eyes I've ever seen. We were inseparable. Most of my days were spent racing over the moss-bordered paths along the lazy, winding river.

"When I was seven we moved to a red brick house in the country, about thirty-five minutes' drive from the city. There my livestock

18

increased considerably. I had ducks, lambs, and three fat little pigs. Our gardener, a marvelous old man with a funny white mustache, made a bright red harness and little wagon for me to ride in. I would drive all around the grounds in my pig-driven chariot. It was wonderful until they began to outgrow their garish little harness. After the pigs, I adopted a family of twenty-three ducklings. They were my first real heartbreak. I remember the terrible morning I woke up and found that some thief had stolen every one of them. My tears were uncontrollable, but mother was so understanding.

"By now, I was beginning to appreciate my mother and all her efforts to give me a fine cultural start in life. Before I had only taken her for granted, like most children do with their parents. But suddenly Mother became a real person to me. I loved her more than I did all the little girls I met at school. I enjoyed being with her more than with any other person, even my playmates—we had so much fun together.

"Most of my childhood was spent playing with my pets. I loved dogs, and still do. Relatives and friends used to give me dolls, but I was never interested in them; in fact I never liked toys of any kind. The only doll that I did cherish was Isabelle, a lovely china doll with painted curls. It had been my mother's when she was a child, and she had saved it in hopes of having a daughter to give it to. Isabelle was my second big heartbreak. One day I had taken her downstairs to show her to friends of my mother's. There were two women in the living room sitting and talking to Mother. I handed my prize possession to one of the women and she examined the doll and started to give it to the other woman when it dropped and smashed into a hundred pieces. I can still feel the way my stomach fell as I looked at Isabelle, hopelessly lost on the floor. She had been my one and only play doll. I gathered up the pieces, almost unable to see them through my tears, and wrapped them in tissue paper—and still have them today.

"I guess I was an unusual child. I never really cared about children of my own age, probably because my family was so close. I learned to depend on myself and my family for fun and companionship. Clothes didn't interest me, in fact I hated to have Mother buy new dresses and things for me. I dressed very simply, and had one dress that I wanted to wear all the time.

"When I was nine, I was invited to a birth-day party, and Mother went out and bought me a lovely new dress—a soft blue color in a gauzy material. She helped me to dress that day, but before I went to the party I went up-stairs and changed into an old favorite. Mother was upset, but I explained that I wanted to have a good time, and couldn't in a new dress. She seemed to understand. I wore the old one and had a marvelous time. In fact that party was memorable because a little boy came up to me and said that I was pretty and he would kiss me. But before he could carry out his threat, I boxed him in the nose so hard that his nose started to bleed. I was proud of my conquest and boasted about it for weeks, much to the poor little boy's horror."

The early years flew swiftly by at the Carpenter home at 3344 Olive Street in Kansas City, and the tow-headed daughter of one of Kansas City's wealthiest dentists grew into a lovely girl. When she was ten years old and attending the very proper Barstow School in Kansas City, the trouble that had been build-ing in the Carpenter home burst into irrepara-ble explosion.

Her parents separated, and Mrs. Carpenter made a fateful decision. She and her blooming

daughter moved to Hollywood, already, in
1921, the film capital of the world—but a
silent one then. The advent of "talkies" would
mean everything to Harlean some seven years
later.

In Hollywood, Harlean was enrolled in the
Hollywood School for Girls, where her classmates were the daughters of famous film actors
and actresses. The atmosphere in which she
would flourish surrounded her like a fable
from the Arabian Nights, and Harlean even
then harkened to the siren song of the movies.

Studies she cared little about, but the tales
told by her classmates about their illustrious
parents, and the visits to the sets, carried Harlean into a tinsel world that inflamed her imagination.

This was no routine Kansas City!

Suddenly, her world was transformed into
a land of marvels, where Sinbad and his Geni,
Cleopatra and Scheherazade, Ben Hur and
dancing houris were real, and the workaday
world outside was of little account. Her impressionable years of eleven, twelve and thir-
teen were spent in this magic world, years in
which memory is vivid, gripping, leaving im-
prints that never fade. It was the era of the
silents, and comedy was king. Hal Roach and

Mack Sennett outdid each other in slapstick episodes which are still classics, and Harlean was herself to become a great comedienne. The breathless blonde adolescent haunted the back lots of Paramount, Fox and Universal, and would one day appear in one of Roach's pie-throwing bruhahas.

No more fantastic world can be imagined than Hollywood during these years, when Douglas Fairbanks, Sr., vaulted balustrades in such epics as *The Mark of Zorro*, *Robin Hood* and *The Three Musketeers*; when Fairbanks' fairytale marriage to Mary Pickford, on March 28, 1920, was celebrated on a scale which can only be called royal; when Charlie Chaplin and Buster Keaton were the presiding comedy geniuses. Harlean suffered a bad case of stardust.

After three years, Harlean was taken by her mother back East to Illinois. But she would be back before long, and not as a stranger.

What she brought back from that glittering Eldorado-by-the-Sea can only be guessed at now, but the tug of Hollywood, like the moon moving the tides, would draw Harlean back, barely three years later, to a strange destiny.

In Illinois, Harlean and her mother made their home in Highland Park, an exclusive and plush suburb of Chicago. Harlean eventually was enrolled in Ferry Hall, a fashionable school for girls in nearby suburban Lake Forest.

Though still only barely on the threshold of adolescence, the girl already bloomed with the tender beginnings of what was to blossom later into stunning physical beauty. Hardly a passerby failed to marvel at the breathtaking vitality of the striking and exuberant youngster as she hurried through the quiet streets of the town on her way to school or to meet friends.

And Harlean did have many friends. A born extrovert, she was quick to surround herself with company, quick to reach out for the fullness of life.

But even at this early stage, the mercurial qualities that later were to mark her meteoric and fairytale movie career began to make themselves evident. Docile as she was in her unfettered friendliness with everyone in her carefree playful world, Harlean balked at the burdensome regimentation of classroom studies.

While her more intense school sisters listened seriously and attentively to their instructors, the academic scene left Harlean cold.

Even the most intriguing subjects under class-room discussion would escape the notice of the daydreaming young beauty as she sat at her desk, chin in hand, her eyes wandering to the window and the big wide world outside.

"And what is your answer, Harlean?" an instructor would ask, piercing through suddenly into the mooning youngster's world of cottony thoughts, only to evoke a flustered, giggly response from a girl who hadn't even heard the question.

But her winning smile and sweet disposition were always enough to save her from any but the most gentle scolding for inattentiveness. Then, having dodged out of her predicament, she promptly returned to her world of dreams.

As a doting and dutiful parent, Harlean's mother was not always so understanding of her daughter's casual attitude toward school work.

Eying report cards that reflected Harlean's less than enthusiastic interest in learning, the mother often tried to have serious discussions with the girl about the importance of knowledge. "You'll have to try harder, Harlean," she often urged. "These studies are very important. You'll need them later on in life. It may not seem that way to you now, but someday you'll see. Someday you'll mark my words."

Harlean was tolerant of these parental lectures and dealt with them in superb theatrical style. A look of astonished and contrite innocence would shine in her eyes and she would brush her lips across her mother's cheek in an affectionate kiss, promising: "I'll try to do better, Mother. I don't mean to hurt you. I know it's important to you, and I'll try."

These poignant domestic scenes happened again and again, in a seemingly endless series, as the girl quickly reverted to type in her wildly impractical, rainbow-chasing way.

Part of her determination to be distracted was due to that most fascinating discovery that all adolescent girls are bound to make sooner or later—boys!

Indeed, it was a very large part. And with her ample qualities of magnetic attraction, Harlean found that she had to expend practically no effort at all to make boys discover her. They flocked around her like bees hovering about a honeycomb.

At first, her contacts with the opposite sex were the frivolous flirtations of any young girl taking her first uncertain steps toward feminine maturity, fraught with interludes of awkwardness, shyness, embarrassment.

If Harlean found these initial unsure explorations into the world of boys somewhat painful and bewildering, her admirers found them even more so. They struggled in all their youthful wonderment to hide their eager feelings. But it was the kind of burning adulation that is not easily veiled, and Harlean could hardly escape noticing that she was indeed the focal point, the center of attraction for gangling swains.

She could hardly be oblivious, either, to the envy this generated in her less enticing sisters. She became a "must" guest at the frequent weekend-night house parties thrown by friends.

There were the usual "post office" and "spin-the-bottle" games that inevitably ornament teenage get-togethers. Of course Harlean —to the undisguised dismay of her girl friends —became the most sought-after object of affection.

This even led on one occasion to a rather sticky party scene in which one of her best friends—throwing caution to the winds—suggested that a kissing game was not being played quite fairly since Harlean seemed to be in it more often than not. It caused quite a bit of consternation among the participants, but Harlean—still not too sophisticated about the power of her beauty—later tried to soothe her friend's embittered feelings, without too much success.

As unaffected as she was about her appearance, Harlean nonetheless sensed its value in the eyes of others. That was a great support for her ego. It was also unreal. Never having come to grips with the stark reality of disapproval and rejection, the girl was soon thrust into the storybook role of the young goddess at whose feet all men swoon in awe.

The sense of challenge and of pursuit that fires most young girls with enthusiasm in the boy-meets-girl realm began ever so faintly to lose out to the axiom that what can be had so easily is rarely very desirable.

But whatever disillusionment or disenchantment she may have experienced with her steady stream of suitors was short-lived. Her feelings of excitement and desire were swiftly reborn the second she laid eyes on a darkly handsome young man at a dance at Ferry Hall one balmy spring night.

They darted quick glances at each other from opposite sides of the crowded dance floor, and it was immediately apparent that both liked what they saw.

Within a very few minutes, both had cleverly maneuvered into speaking distance and the young man had asked, "Would you like to dance?"

Soon they were caught up in the swirl of dancing couples, and pretty much caught up in each other, as their gay conversation revealed that they had a great deal in common.

That night, Charles "Chuck" Freemont McGrew 3rd, twenty-two-year-old bond broker and scion of a wealthy Chicago family, took Harlean home and left her glowing from a goodnight kiss.

In the weeks and months that followed, a whirlwind romance blossomed as Harlean and Chuck became practically inseparable at parties, dances, picnics. Then there were the long solitary walks through the dark, deserted streets of Highland Park, late at night and sometimes into the predawn hours, during which they exchanged—as do all young couples in love—their innermost thoughts and ambitions in life.

The parents on both sides of the affair grew anxious as it became increasingly apparent that the two were destined to make their relationship permanent.

But perhaps the most concerned was Harlean's mother when her daughter, radiant with happiness, burst into their home one night to announce: "I'm in love with Chuck and I want to marry him."

After gathering herself together from the shock of the announcement, the mother sternly advised: "How can you get married? You're still only a baby. What do you know about life? Why, you have your whole life ahead of you. You're not ready to settle down."

What the mother said was true—Harlean was now only sixteen years old—but reality is seldom a part of the world of a young woman adrift in a sea of romantic emotion.

Harlean received the words of parental wisdom with a mixture of disappointment and anger. They failed to dim her ardor and her determination to become Chuck McGrew's bride. However, to avoid her mother's wrath, she said nothing, but slipped off that very night to discuss the matter at a secret rendezvous with her beloved, who also had experienced some resistance from his family.

Locked in each other's arms and linked by those irrepressible emotions that simply cannot be either explained or denied, the couple hit upon a solution that seemed the only easy way out of their perplexing problem. Their thoughts immediately turned to a quick answer. Within a few hours they were en route to Waukegan—a town where the principal, or at least best known, stock in trade was quickie marriages.

The only possible obstacle in the headlong rush to tie the marital knot was Harlean's age.

A justice of the peace eyed her somewhat warily when she stated, in answer to a question on the marriage license application, that she was born on March 30, 1908.

By this time, however, Harlean's mature appearance was more than enough to carry off the fib. So, in the sunlit parlor of the jurist's home, with a couple of aged townsfolk standing in as witnesses, Harlean and Chuck became man and wife.

Chapter Three

Many marriages end whatever family opposition there might have been to a match, but it was not true in this case. Trouble continued, and Harlean and Chuck solved it by fleeing to Beverly Hills to start their married life in a Spanish bungalow.

But the bond between Harlean and her mother was not easily broken. Her mother, who had remarried and was now Mrs. Marino Bello, wife of a former Chicago hotel man, followed the newlyweds to California. Thus the stage was finally set.

Harlean's marriage was doomed from the start, mainly because of her immaturity. At first all went well, since her mother and stepfather forgave the runaways and accepted the marriage. Ironically, Harlean herself wasn't able to accept it. Very soon she and Chuck separated, and after the divorce she moved in with her mother. At seventeen, Harlean had put her first tragedy behind her.

Now the lovely blonde went out socially in Hollywood, attending numerous parties among movie people. How, exactly, she drifted into movie-making is uncertain, because there are at least two seemingly reliable versions—one from Mrs. Bello and one from Harlean herself.

The first version is that Harlean, an inveterate gambler already, took a $250 bet that she could get a part in a movie if she wanted one—which she said she really didn't. She had visited a studio one day and claimed she was asked if she would like to be in pictures.

"I told them no," she laughed later, but she appeared pleased.

"You couldn't get a part anyway," a friend taunted.

Jean, who later made almost legendary strikes at gambling at Agua Caliente, and whose proudest boast would become that she held the record of 34 straight passes at a dice table, was equal to the challenge.

"It's a bet," she laughed.

And so, Harlean registered with the Central Casting Bureau, and a few weeks later got a bit part as a $15-a-day extra in Clara Bow's *The Saturday Night Kid*. The legend is that Harlean was still married at this time, and that Chuck opposed the movie fling. After winning her bet, Harlean dropped the whole thing and forgot about the movies.

After her divorce, however, she again registered with Central Casting and appeared as a bit player in *Paramount Parade*, a Hal Roach pie-throwing comedy, and in *Moran of the Marines*, in which her part was so trifling that if one blinked he missed her altogether.

By now Harlean had adopted her mother's maiden name and was, at last, Jean Harlow.

Apparently Jean didn't take it all very seriously, even after the few first bits, and it was not until a family friend who was also a great actress came to her home one day that a future in the movies began to assume any real meaning for her.

"You're going places," the actress told Jean. "Just as sure as my name is Marie Dressler."

Miss Dressler persuaded Hal Roach to sign Jean to a contract, and several comedies followed, none memorable. But revolution was shaking the movie industry, just in time for

Jean Harlow.

In 1927, Al Jolson's *The Jazz Singer* had brought panic to Hollywood. Al sang and talked, and although it wasn't exactly evident overnight, the "silents" were dead. At that time a young Texas tycoon named Howard Hughes had a million-dollar headache on his hands. He had just completed the greatest of all World War I movies, *Hell's Angels*. And it was "silent."

What to do?

The film, as made, starred Greta Nissen, a Norwegian beauty from Oslo who was easy to look at but who spoke only broken English. In the silents she was gorgeous; in the talkies, ridiculous.

Jean had previously met Ben Lyon and James Hall, who were featured in *Hell's Angels*, and she persuaded them to ask Hughes to give her a chance. She got the chance, got the role, and became an overnight sensation.

The other version of how she broke into the movies was that her mother, as some society women did then, had herself signed up at Central Casting. She was called for a café scene in a movie called *Masquerade*, being made on the old Fox lot at Sunset Boulevard and Western Avenue, under the direction of Russell J.

Birdwell.

Mrs. Bello timidly asked Director Birdwell if she might bring her daughter along. "I wonder if you'd mind if I brought my little girl on the set with me?" was her ingenuous question.

"All right," Birdwell said indulgently, "bring the little girl with you tomorrow."

The "little girl" walked onto the set the next day and hit Director Birdwell like a ton of bricks.

"She was the most flawlessly beautiful young woman I had ever seen," the entranced director said.

He promptly signed her too as an extra, and she worked four days in *Masquerade*.

From there, the second version agrees with the first. Ben Lyon and James Hall steered Jean to Howard Hughes—and to immortality.

But in those first few meetings with the energetic young producer, Jean suffered the same reaction that Hughes' forceful personality imposed on most people. She was terrified.

Hughes was as canny and shrewd as he was frightening to a young, inexperienced actress. He knew instinctively that Harlow was born for the role in *Hell's Angels*, yet he realized that one of the cardinal rules in negotiating was never to show anxiousness, never to tip your hand. When he first confronted Jean, he stared at her hard and coldly for a few seconds, then began shaking his head slowly. Harlow's heart sank.

"Skinny," he muttered, "and that hair. What the hell kind of hair is that?" Again he shook his head. He looked hard at her again and walked away.

The screen test itself was rather simple. It lasted just four minutes on film. In it, Miss Harlow appeared in a simple robe and sat at a dressing table, facing the camera. There was no script. No lines to memorize. There was no real acting involved. Jean sat at the table and simply talked about anything that came into her mind. Yet despite the simple demands of the test, she was nervous. For one thing, she knew how much was riding on the outcome. For another, it's often quite difficult to ad lib, to talk extemporaneously, particularly when some display of emotion is called for.

But in spite of the difficulties, Jean came through magnificently. She smiled at the cameras, did engaging little things with her hands. She lit a cigarette. She teased a lock of hair. She patted her chin jokingly. She tugged at the neckline of her robe. She talked informally throughout the four minutes, and through all the talk, the gestures, came a girl of fantastic allure. Everything seemed to accent her tremendous physical charm. Howard Hughes ran and reran the screen test, studied it again and again, and when he was through he knew he had his star.

Hell's Angels was rewritten with dialogue suited to Jean Harlow's personality, and was completed in a short time. It had its world premiere in New York, in a Broadway theater, and Jean went to New York for the opening. The advance publicity given *Hell's Angels* had already thrust Jean Harlow's image into the public's consciousness. The phrase "platinum blonde" had already entered the language. Even before the picture premiered, the rush was on by millions of young girls across the continent to get some hair dye. The rush would reach almost stampede proportions months later, after 70 million people had seen *Hell's Angels*.

The movie's premiere was Jean Harlow's introduction to New York, and specifically to Broadway. She'd never been farther East than Chicago before this.

The big town captivated her. And she captivated it. Thousands of fans turned out for the premiere, more to see the sexy new star with the incredible platinum blonde hair than to see the picture of World War I air heroes.

Her impact on the public was virtually unprecedented. No other movie queen in memory had ever transfixed the paying public the way Harlow did. Some others imprinted their personalities, or beauty, on the public in dramatic fashion, but none as vividly as Harlow. Possibly the only others comparable—but not quite equal—to Jean's impact were Theda Bara and Greta Garbo. But Harlow was supreme. Her success in *Hell's Angels* was instantaneous. As she left the theater after the premiere, the crowds pressed about her. Hands reached out, hoping to touch her. She was swamped with requests for autographs. Policemen had to form a cordon around her to keep the throngs back. Afterward, at a party, dozens of champagne toasts were drunk to her.

Harlow went to a succession of parties, big and small, during her stay in New York, and became the darling of the press. Every paper in town wanted an interview with the new love goddess of Hollywood, the "platinum blonde." Harlow saw them all. Everything was intoxicating. She went to the great fashionable shops on famed Fifth Avenue, and by the time she was ready to return to Hollywood, she'd purchased exactly 31 new dresses, shoes to match each, furs, jewelry and a raft of other accessories. She even hired a secretary.

Back in Hollywood, Harlow expected to rush immediately into work again for Hughes, who, she reasoned, would want to take advantage of her great success and follow through with another picture certain to be a big money-maker. But she was disappointed. There was no picture waiting for her. Nor did any come along in the following weeks. She was crestfallen. She had come to admire Hughes, respect his judgment, rely on him. But for some reason, he seemed to be ignoring her.

Instead of assigning her to one of his own pictures, he began instead to loan her to other studios. Actually, the loan-outs helped reassure her of her momentous success. When word got around that Jean Harlow was available—that Hughes was willing to negotiate her services—the major studios began bidding furiously for her.

She did a quick succession of films, all of them taking advantage of the peculiar, original style of comedy Harlow was so good at. Immediately after *Hell's Angels* she cranked out

Iron Man, The Secret Six, The Public Enemy, Goldie, and *The Beast of the City.* Her leading men included such charming males as Lew Ayres, James Cagney, Ben Lyon, Wallace Beery, Robert Taylor, Clark Gable, Spencer Tracy and Walter Huston.

Each new film carried the Harlow skyrocket farther into the firmament of wealth and fame.

She was seen constantly with a parade of handsome leading men, at parties, at dinners, horseback riding, at the beach. Part of it was the continuing build-up each producer or studio wanted her to have. Part of it was simply that Jean Harlow was then the toast of Hollywood, the most desired girl in town and probably in the world.

Yet despite the dates and the constant admiration, Jean's private life was becoming a little messy.

The divorce proceedings against her estranged husband, Charles McGrew, were getting bogged down. A default had been entered into the court, making hers an uncontested divorce suit.

But now McGrew was showing a renewed interest in Jean, and evidently decided he wanted to keep her as his wife. He filed an action to set aside the default on the grounds that he was drunk at the time the papers were served. Therefore, he argued in his new legal action, the default wasn't binding. Whether or not he thought that by fighting the divorce he might get Jean back is uncertain. But Jean did fight back, determined to win the divorce. At that point, McGrew became bitter once more and counter-filed for his own divorce.

In addition to claiming he was drunk at the time he signed the temporary agreement, he accused Jean of posing for indecent pictures and for beginning a screen career without his consent.

Full details of McGrew's charges were never made public, but it was understood the pictures he was talking about were still photos of Jean in the nude or semi-nude. He made the accusation in a civil suit answering Jean's appeal for $4,500 Jean claimed McGrew owed her under the old temporary agreement, signed in 1929 when they first separated.

Jean replied to all the charges. It was true, she said, that McGrew had arrived at her home intoxicated at 4 A.M. one day to tell her he was flying out of town in order to avoid being served with any papers. While she talked to him, her mother called the process servers, and the papers were served on McGrew as he was leaving. But, Jean argued, that was the only time drunkenness entered into the proceedings. McGrew was not drunk when he actually signed the agreement, she said.

As for the charge that she went into the movies against his wishes, Jean stated: "As far as my husband's objections to my movie career are concerned, this is ridiculous. I was compelled by him to make my own living, due to his refusal to support me."

And finally, in answer to McGrew's charge that Jean had posed for indecent pictures, the actress declared coldly: "The photographs referred to were the work of Edwin Bower Hesser, the well-known artist-photographer of Hollywood, and were made at the request of Mr. and Mrs. Hesser, who invited my husband and me to accompany them to the mountains for an outing. These photographs of me, posed by Mr. and Mrs. Hesser, were taken of me as a draped wood nymph and were to be used for publication purposes by the artist."

Simply put, they were publicity pictures showing her in a flowing gown.

The legal actions dragged out for almost a year. Finally, when the difficulties were all ironed out, Jean got her divorce, in January

1931. The settlement gave her the money McGrew owed her, plus alimony of $375 a month, an automobile, and the Beverly Hills house. But Harlow gave back everything. She only wanted a moral victory, she explained later.

In her professional life, things were moving ahead meteorically. The films were being rushed out one after another, solidifying her position as the top box-office draw in Hollywood and enhancing her reputation as a comedienne.

But Jean was becoming dissatisfied, despite her huge successes.

She wanted more money. And she wanted a variety of roles. She had no grand pretensions toward heavy drama; she wasn't foolish enough to believe her talent was great enough to carry off a Portia or a Juliet. But she did want some other roles than that of the sexy vamp or the gold digger. She was becoming stereotyped in the public's mind, and she didn't like it.

"I'd like to get a few things straightened out," she told an interviewer about that time. "I know I play—well, uneducated roles on the screen. But I would like everyone to know that I can read, and that I know which fork to use. I can pronounce *pâté de fois gras*, and I can speak English. It may not be the king's English, but it's good English."

She realized, she said, that she could never play ingenue roles, but she added wistfully, "I do hope that sometime I can bring to the screen a good girl with a streak of badness or a bad girl with a streak of goodness. Something with more range than the pictures I've been getting."

Jean was seeing a lot of interviewers during that time. She would usually set aside a whole day and talk to members of the press, one at a time, from morning till night. It would usually be in her dressing room, all white and green with little honey-colored bear rugs scattered around the floor. She would flounce in, usually in slacks and a sweater or a short-sleeved blouse, and drop into the apple-green couch in the room. Then the action would begin. She would constantly shift position, cross and uncross her famous legs, toss her hair back, possibly get up and look out the window, and drag constantly on the ever-present cigarette. She would talk candidly and answer all questions, including the silly ones:

"What's your favorite color?"

"Green."

"What's your favorite food?"

"Hamburgers."

And so on.

Because of the tremendous amount of publicity she received, she became something of a national institution.

That year—1931—a hairdressers' convention used "platinum hair" as its convention theme. In dress shops throughout the land, "Harlow" styles mushroomed—tight-fitting dresses, usually, with low necklines. Jean Harlow dolls for little girls appeared in toy shops and department stores everywhere. When Jean took up dieting, the whole country dieted, and everyone wanted to know what she was eating. When it became known that Harlow was taking ballet lessons, thousands of young girls—and some not so young, too—enrolled in ballet classes hoping to emulate her. As it happened, the ballet lessons were an accident for Jean. She'd been taking some routine dancing lessons for a picture—simple little time steps for a tap routine—but some of the exercises were really ballet exercises to toughen her legs. After two weeks, Jean noticed that her silhouette was taking on a new shape. And she liked it. Comparing her measurements one morning, she found:

Before dancing:
Bust—34
Hips—37
Waist—24
After dancing:
Bust—33
Hips—36
Waist—23

While she hardly needed to lose weight—she was five feet three and 113 pounds—the loss of four pounds by dancing pleased her, and she kept up the ballet exercises long after she finished the picture.

Her physical fitness was, in fact, a matter of importance to her. She knew she wouldn't be where she was without her physical charm, and she worked at keeping in the best condition possible.

"Beauty," she said, "is a twenty-four hour a day job. It allows no time off. It means self-denial and downright work. But it's worth it. Once you make a set of rules for yourself, never break them. Take my diet, for instance. I never vary it from day to day—unless I'm absolutely dying for a hamburger. For breakfast I have fruit juice, coffee, dry toast and an occasional soft-boiled egg. For lunch I have a cup of clear vegetable soup. For dinner I have two vegetables, a salad, meat or cottage cheese and fruit."

Besides the ballet exercises, Jean went in for sports strenuously to help keep her shape in trim. She played golf and tennis, rode horseback, went swimming in her pool every day, and relaxed under a massage twice a week.

The public hungered for the intimate details of Jean Harlow's existence, and Jean, aware of the interest, fed her secrets out through the press in a constant stream of interviews. It was all part of being a "star," of being larger than life to her admiring fans, of fulfilling the obligation to be glamorous.

And of course it was paying off. She was the darling of the vast movie-going public, and in demand by every studio in Hollywood.

About this time, Harlow gave the first full-fledged interview that set the record straight about her start in the movies, and some of the subsequent events.

"The first contact I had with motion pictures was accidentally through a girl I met at a party, another young bride like myself," she began. "Her name was Lucille Lee and she had occasionally played in motion pictures, just bit parts. I went to a luncheon with her one afternoon and suddenly in the midst of the meal she said she had to rush away to keep an interview appointment at Fox Studios. It sounded so exciting, and I asked her if she could take me through the studio gates. She said yes, if I would drive her there.

"I drove Lucille there, and waited outside. It was intriguing—all the people, the streets, the buildings, and the bustling traffic of a busy studio. When Lucille came out, there were three men with her, and she introduced me. They seemed very interested, and asked me if I had ever entertained any ambitions to crash the movie gates. I told them frankly that I hadn't. Then they told me that if I did ever consider it, they would give me a note of introduction to the casting director of the General Casting Bureau, the clearing house for all new-comers who want careers in pictures.

"I took the letters, drove home, put them in the desk drawer, and promptly forgot them. Weeks later at a party, the conversation got around to movies, and a couple of my friends bet me that I didn't have the nerve to take the letters and apply for work in pictures.

"Next day, just to win the bet, I put on my best dress and went down to Fox Studios. I registered at the Central Casting Bureau, and had a long talk with a casting director at Fox.

When I got home, I called my friends and told them that they had lost the bet. Then I thought the whole thing was finished.

"I was so surprised when I began to receive calls for work as an extra player. At first I refused, using all sorts of excuses. Then, just for the fun of it, I went to work as an extra in a Fox picture.

"It was like a dream. Everyone was so lovely and willing to help me. A few days later I accepted a call for a longer job. This time I worked several days as 'atmosphere' with Richard Dix and Ruth Elder in a Paramount picture, *Moran of the Marines*. After that calls came from other studios. The casting director of the Hal Roach Studios had seen the few feet of film I had done for Fox, and offered me two short comedies and a five-year contract to play leading roles with the Roach comedians.

"By now, of course, the lure of motion pictures was in my blood. I had won screen credit in two short comedies—*Whoopee* and *The Unkissed Man*. Suddenly, from just 'atmosphere,' I was playing a leading lady, even if only in two-reel comedies.

"My affairs at home were not doing as well as my career. Chuck and I were beginning to realize that we had been too young to think of marriage, that our ideas of life did not agree. The pictures were a welcome cure for my mental unrest, and I signed a five-year contract with the Hal Roach Studios. At that point, Chuck and I agreed on a friendly separation. He returned to Chicago and I went to my mother and stepfather's home.

"The one thing I had forgotten to do was inform my grandparents of my plans for the future, and one night I received a frantic telephone call from them from Kansas City. It was Grandfather, so emotionally upset that he was almost unable to talk coherently. It seems that that night he and my grandmother had gone to the movies, and had witnessed their loving granddaughter prancing across the screen in a filmy black lace nightie.

"It had almost shattered my grandfather's heart to see me, his lovable granddaughter, 'flaunting herself in diaphanous underthings.' Futhermore, he had been shocked to find that I had adopted my mother's name—Jean Harlow—for such a public career. The result was that I promised to give up my screen career and settle down quietly to be just Harlean Carpenter again. Next day, with tears running down my cheeks, I explained the whole thing to Hal Roach, and he released me from the five-year contract.

"When I went home to my mother's house, I thought my screen career was over forever. I felt very sad, and for eight months did almost nothing, living a quiet uneventful life. I saw only one or two friends, and tried to break the monotony by riding horseback over the Beverly Hills bridal paths and swimming in the cool surf of the Pacific . . . but I was restless. I wanted activity. I had smelled grease paint, and was unable to forget it. I had to get back into the absorbing life of make-believe.

"One day, when all hope had just about vanished, I received a call to play a small bit with Clara Bow in *The Saturday Night Kid*. I couldn't resist the urge, so I dusted off my makeup kit and accepted the job. After that I worked in a few short pictures at the Christie Studio, where I met Ben Lyon and Jimmy Hall. Both were working for Howard Hughes in *Hell's Angels*, which had started as a silent picture but was being remade because of the arrival of the talkies. Greta Nissen, the original leading lady, was in New York and couldn't return to Hollywood to play in the new version.

"Ben and Jimmy decided to take me over

to the Caddo Studios and introduce me to Hughes. I took a test for the leading role, and got it. It was such great luck, I still can't explain why it happened. But before I accepted the role, I telephoned my grandfather and had a long heart-to-heart talk with him. I told him the truth, as he had always taught me to. I told him how pictures were the only absorbing interest in my life, and that I just had to go to work, and this was my big chance. He really understood me, and finally gave his consent, which cleared my heart and my conscience.

"Everything broke loose with that picture. It seemed to have made a sensational hit in Hollywood, and me along with it. The world premiere at Grauman's Chinese Theater was like a dream to me. I couldn't believe that the platinum-haired girl who greeted the milling populace over the microphone, who was feted and dined that memorable night, was once little Harlean Carpenter of Kansas City.

"After the success of *Hell's Angels*, Howard Hughes gave me a long-term contract, but I never again worked for Caddo Studios. They loaned me out to play in pictures at other studios. Somehow the most terrible blow of all, after my sudden success, was that I was 'typed.' I was the hard-boiled siren, and no one

54

would give me a chance to play any other kind of role. Months passed, and I really became discouraged. I wanted to prove that I could play other things besides a platinum-haired vamp.

"Somehow I hoped to bring to the screen a good girl with a streak of badness, or a bad girl with a sprinkling of goodness. Each night, after a day of 'vamping' at the studio, I would go home and pour out my sorrows and disappointments to my mother and stepfather. I didn't know what to do. At last I got a tempting offer to make a personal appearance tour across the country. The Caddo Studio gave their consent, and I was delighted to leave Hollywood, where I had become very unhappy.

"My mother and stepfather and I traveled around the country for a year and a half, playing four, sometimes five shows a day. It was exhausting, but when we reached New York, my golden opportunity came. Metro-Goldwyn-Mayer wanted me for a picture, and I was delighted. It was called *The Secret Six*, and George Hill was directing it. Wallace Beery was in it, and a rising newcomer, Clark Gable.

"My stepfather convinced my mother and

me to move to a beautiful English Tudor home high on one of Hollywood's romantic hilltops. From my bedroom windows I could see a panorama of the Pacific and the glistening peaks of Los Angeles' downtown buildings. Everything was going well and we were all very happy."

Chapter Four

Howard Hughes was still not using Harlow, despite the fact that he still held her contract. Jean signed next to do *Red-Headed Woman* for Metro-Goldwyn-Mayer. She signed for it during her second trip back East for publicity purposes. She exclaimed happily to the press, her platinum locks flying as she laughed, "At last! I've got a chance to be a girl with a new color of hair!"

Jean came back to Hollywood and plunged into production. Her co-star was the biggest male box-office attraction of the time—big, rugged Clark Gable. They'd worked once before together, in *The Secret Six*.

Red-Headed Woman brought someone else

back into Jean's life—a man she'd met three years earlier at a cocktail party while she was still an extra, and whom she'd come to know by reputation in the years since.

His name was Paul Bern, and he was to become her second husband not long after the completion of *Red-Headed Woman*.

Bern was production supervisor at M-G-M and in over-all charge of shooting the new Harlow picture. He was a small, shy man, but a genius at his craft. In many ways he and Jean Harlow were the complete antithesis of one another. Harlow embodied everything that was glamorous, outgoing. Bern's whole character was just the opposite. He was aesthetic, introverted. Harlow was the performer. Bern, in his way, was the creator. Harlow, though not loud in the brassy sense of the word, was vivacious, ebullient. Bern was quiet. Harlow was a high laugh, head thrown back. Bern was a soft, private smile.

Yet they were attracted to each other almost from the moment shooting began on *Red-Headed Woman*. On his part, Bern admired the private side of Harlow. Unlike the public, he did not confuse Jean Harlow the woman with Jean Harlow, the girl on the screen. He saw Jean not as a vamplike, hard-boiled gold digger with a quick funny answer to everything, but as a sensitive and somewhat insecure young woman who created the screen character to conceal a genuinely shy personality. For her part, Jean admired Bern for his genius, for his soft ways, for the interest he showed her mind.

In that respect she was responding to Paul Bern's personality much as everyone who knew him responded. He was a modest, cultured gentleman who shunned the false hilarity, the hectic revelry of Hollywood. He attended none of the large, glittering parties the great screen luminaries found it fashionable to stage periodically. His attitude toward Hollywood was introspective; his genius was that he saw motion pictures not only as box-office returns but as an art form.

He became known in Hollywood, particularly around the M-G-M lot, as "Hollywood's Father Confessor." His hand was always offered in help to those who needed it; he shared their joys, their sorrows. Sympathy was Bern's chief characteristic. His sensitive nature seemed to attune him to the sorrows and sufferings of others, and he seemed almost compelled to make any sacrifice for a friend.

He opened both his heart and his pocket-book to everyone—a fading star, an aspiring extra, the cameraman who had come upon hard times. When the world turned a cold shoulder on some unfortunate soul, he was the first to the rescue.

Some of the stories about Bern and the way he helped others became part of the Hollywood legend.

There was the case of actress Barbara La Marr, once a great personal friend of Bern's and the girl he was frequently linked to romantically before Harlow. Poverty-stricken, Barbara La Marr was at death's door from a lingering illness. All the fair-weather friends she'd made when she was an actress had now abandoned her.

But Bern bought her a home in Altadena and summoned Los Angeles' foremost doctors to attend her. He saw to it that nurses were always in attendance. And he himself was there, in deep grief, when death finally came to her.

Lovely Mabel Normand, another actress who'd come upon hard times, also found Bern loyal to her to the end. She became involved in the mystery surrounding the slaying of a man named William Desmond Taylor. Throughout her ordeal, Bern shielded her and finally used his influence to force other Hollywood executives to hire her, despite the scandal she'd been in. To the day of her death, Miss Normand was grateful. And when death overtook her, the man she'd called her best friend stood and watched the fresh green earth cover her casket.

Nor were they the only ones. Bern had a special sympathy for foreign artists, people who found the customs of Hollywood strange and even barbaric. Nita Naldi sought and received his advice, and so did Rudolph Valentino, the great romantic lead during Hollywood's early days. And another dashing hero of the day, Ramon Novarro, considered him almost like a brother.

There were still others. The well-known star John Gilbert was guided throughout his stormy career by Paul Bern. The great star of a generation earlier, Wallace Reid, said he would be indebted to Bern for life for the help Bern gave him. And so it was, always. No one was too unimportant to ask for and receive aid from the gentle Bern.

Bern's career was, in its way, as meteoric as Jean Harlow's. He was born in Wandsbeck, Germany, in 1890, one of 18 children.

Brought to New York when he was nine,

Bern got his early education in the city's public schools while he grew up in New York's then melting pot area, the teaming tenement district known as the Lower East Side. After completing high school, he worked his way through a business college, and still later won a scholarship to a dramatic school. From early adulthood on his chief interest was in the direction of the theater. Between 1911 and 1914, he was an actor, stage manager, director and producer with stock companies at Glens Falls, New York; Woonsocket, Rhode Island; Denver, Colorado; and Wilmington, Delaware.

His first work in motion pictures was with a Canadian company, in 1914. He moved from one company to another in the next four years, learning all there was to know about the infant industry. In 1918 he joined the Goldwyn studio, serving as cutter, assistant director and scenarist. Later he worked as a producer, turning out, among others, *Open All Night*, *The Dressmaker of Paris*, and *Flower of the Night*.

With each picture, his reputation grew, not only as a brilliant executive but as a warm human being who could get the most from his actors and actresses. Subsequently, he was signed by Metro-Goldwyn-Mayer to direct four pictures a year at an annual salary of

$35,000. But his value to the studio was so great that within a short time he was made production supervisor, and much of the great success the studio had in those early years was attributable to the genius of Paul Bern.

But there was another side to the man who would one day marry Jean Harlow and, barely two months later, end his life with a bullet in his head. Despite his deep compassion for the troubles of others, he himself had a deprecating view of his own talents, his own personality. He could, at times, be morbid about himself.

His friends around the studio had frequently heard him say that other members of his family had committed suicide, and time and again Bern had discussed the possibility of seeking the answer to his own problems in self-destruction. He often told intimates that he considered it proper for a man to end his life if he felt his existence was no longer justified. He attributed his morbid outlook on life to the fact that, in his early youth in New York, as a member of a poor and large family, he had often gone hungry.

But if he thought little of himself and of his own chances for happiness, he was beloved by the people who knew and worked with him. Before *Red-Headed Woman* was under way more than a week, Jean Harlow had come under his warm spell.

It was Harlow who engineered their first meeting in three years. She'd been back in Hollywood barely a month after finishing her publicity tour in the East, where she'd signed the M-G-M contract to do *Red-Headed Woman*. She'd gone to the M-G-M studios, where sets were still being created and assistant directors were still working on the casting. She spotted a short—just barely as tall as she was—man, thin-haired, almost balding, walking across the studio lot, and she hurried over to him.

"Aren't you Paul Bern?" she asked. "I'm Jean Harlow. I met you three years ago at a party. Do you remember?"

Bern smiled. He of course knew the great star Jean Harlow on sight, but it amused him that she had to remind him of their first meeting. "Certainly I remember, Miss Harlow," he said with the diffidence that was one of his great charms. "How could I forget a person as lovely as you? You've come quite a way since then. I imagine you've learned a good deal about the business. I'd like to talk to you about it sometime."

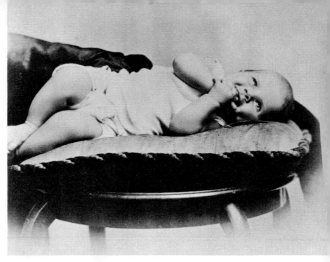

Jean Harlow at six months.

Below at four.

Jean Harlow at the height of her glorious career.

Jean with her second husband, Paul Bern.

Jean Harlow at the age of three.

Jean was always a great believer in physical fitness.

Jean with her mother and stepfather, Mr. & Mrs. Bello.

With Roger Imhoff and Mickey Rooney in "Riff Raff."

A young Jackie Cooper admires Jean's new 12-cylinder.

The essence of sexual sophistication in white satin.

Jean with Dick Powell at a "Hollywood Hotel" broadcast.

With James Cagney in "The Public Enemy."

Jean with Miss Louella Parsons.

With Franchot Tone and Cary Grant in "Suzy."

Jean with Clark Gable in "Hold Your Man."

Jean Harlow and Clark Gable in "Red Dust."

Another scene from "Red Dust."

Jean Harlow with her lovely mother.

With William Powell and Rosalind Russell in "Reckless."

One of the first women in Hollywood to wear slacks.

Sexiness with a sense of humor.

Jean, somewhat plumper, but still beautiful.

Jean with her third husband, Hal Rosson.

With James Stewart in "Wife vs. Secretary."

Jean Harlow in "Dinner at Eight."

Jean with Franchot Tone in "Suzy."

The "Platinum Blonde" reclining.

Jean with Spencer Tracy in "Goldie."

With William Powell in "Reckless."

Jean Harlow with Cary Grant in "Suzy."

Jean with Pat O'Brien in "Bombshell."

With Clark Gable in "Hold Your Man."

With Wallace Beery and Clark Gable in "China Seas."

Jean in a playful mood.

Jean with Spencer Tracy on the set of "Riff Raff."

An early example of Harlow cheesecake.

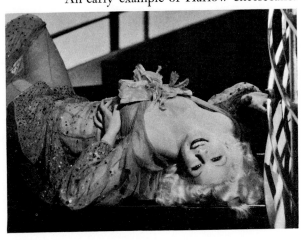

A scene from "Libeled Lady."

She was one of the most beautiful women in the world.

A scene from "Dinner at Eight."

Jean at her most glamorous and with a beauty mark.

A scene from "Wife vs. Secretary."

Jean Harlow with Robert Taylor in "Personal Property."

Miss Harlow at her sultriest.

At her most glamorous in "Dinner at Eight."

Jean with William Powell in "Reckless."

Bern was in a rush for another appointment and had to run off, but just the warmth of that first encounter had its effect on Harlow, and she found herself looking for Bern when the shooting actually began.

At their next meeting, and at subsequent ones, Harlow became absorbed in the modest, retiring executive who seemed to be impervious to her physical charms and dwelt instead on her thoughts, her emotions, her ideas about motion pictures, about life itself, about art, techniques of acting, about happiness, her dreams, her hopes. Not once did he make an overt pass at her. She became intrigued with him. They began having dinner together, not at the garish Hollywood night clubs, but at her home or his, a huge five-acre estate he'd bought five years earlier and that was one of the loveliest places in Beverly Hills.

Their "dates"—if they can be called that—were quiet walks in the evening, enjoying long serious talks in which each plumbed the other's mind. Soon they were constantly together; and then, on July 2, 1932, they were married.

The news shocked Hollywood. First, no one had actually realized the intensity of their relationship. Second, on the surface the match seemed strange, perhaps even ludicrous. Jean

Harlow was the epitome of everything glamorous, the embodiment of the Hollywood ha-cha girl. Bern was exactly the opposite. Marriage between the two seemed improbable at best, disastrous at worst.

There was, additionally, the allegation that Bern was impotent, and virtually everyone in Hollywood, or at least those in his close circle, talked about it. Did Harlow know about this gossip? Author Adela Rogers St. John, years later, shed some light on the subject.

"Barbara La Marr projected me into the middle of Jean Harlow's marriage to Paul Bern," Miss St. John wrote. "Barbara was dead by then, but the things she once told me lived in my memory. Paul had wanted to marry her once upon a time. She refused. The night she married Jack Daugherty, Paul tried to drown himself. Jack Gilbert and Carey Wilson saved him, but there was plenty of gossip about it in Hollywood. It was Barbara who then told me what kind of person Paul was and why she wouldn't marry him."

Miss St. John was referring to Bern's alleged impotency. The announcement of Bern's engagement to Jean Harlow reached print, and Miss St. John continued: "When I went to see Jean after her engagement was announced,

I learned that Paul hadn't told her about himself. I told her.

" 'Then it's true,' she said, and began to cry. 'Paul loves me, as he says he does, for my mind, my spirit, my companionship, for me. He's paid me the highest compliment I've ever had. No man has ever loved me before for what's best in me.'

"So she entered into a marriage that would be a marriage in name only."

Despite the misgivings of their closest friends, Jean and Paul did get married, in the home of Jean's mother. The ceremony was performed by California Superior Judge Leon Yankwich. Actor John Gilbert was best man. It was a simple ceremony, quickly completed. The next day, the newlyweds threw an elaborate reception at Bern's home. Actually, it was now Jean's estate, a lovely two-story European mansion with a beautiful swimming pool. Paul had given it to Jean just before their marriage.

Jean was then in the throes of work, and the couple weren't able to leave on a honeymoon. It didn't seem to matter. They kept to themselves, and seemed, to all outward appearances, to be happy. They continued their long walks, their serious conversations.

But something soon seemed to go wrong. They were seen and heard arguing before they'd been married a month. Little was known of their private life at home as the deterioration began to set in, but by August people were saying, "It can't last."

And it didn't.

It ended with the shocking suicide of Paul Bern in the early morning hours of September 6, 1932, killed by a bullet in the brain.

The suicide was as unexpected as it was shocking, at least to those closest to Paul and Jean. True, they'd seen the Bernses argue occasionally—even more than two people might be expected to who'd only been married two months. But nothing, certainly, indicated Bern was that depressed. He'd been coming to the M-G-M studio daily, putting in long hours of work in a job that required a tremendous amount of concentration on details. He could hardly have continued functioning, they reasoned, if his despondency were so deep. And yet it had to be, for Bern to commit suicide. So the entire movie industry was taken by surprise and stunned at the tragic news.

Jean herself was away at the time, visiting her mother. When she heard about her husband's death, she collapsed into tears, locked herself in a bedroom and, inconsolable with grief, refused to talk to anyone.

Within hours after Bern's body was discovered, the suicide became the Number One topic of conversation. The body was found by the Bernses' butler, an elderly man named John Carmichael. He entered the master bedroom at breakfast time on the morning of July 6 to ask if Bern were ready for breakfast, and instead found his employer lying on the floor, between the bed and the dresser, in a pool of blood.

A gun was in his hand.

On a table next to the bed was a note written in Bern's handwriting and scribbled in a green morocco-bound notebook. It stated, rather cryptically:
"Dearest Dear:

Unfortunately this is the only way to make good the frightful wrong I have done you and to wipe out my abject humility. I love you."

There was a postscript that said: "You understand that last night was only a comedy."

Next to the notebook was a framed photograph of Jean Harlow at her most glamorous.

Carmichael, the butler, notified police and then called Louis B. Mayer at M-G-M studios. Mayer and his top executive Irving Thalberg arrived at the Bern mansion minutes later. They even got there before the police. They could shed little light on the sorrowful death, but Mayer did tell Detective Lieutenant Joseph Whitehead that, "Mr. Thalberg and myself had noticed that Mr. Bern had been extremely nervous lately and we believed he had overworked himself. We had talked about his condition and we were worried."

Both Mayer and Thalberg knew that Jean had stayed that night at her mother's house, and they went there together a short while later. Harlow was still in the bedroom, awake but deeply morose. Precisely what happened has never become publicly known, but reports came out later that while Mayer and Thalberg were there, Jean tried to throw herself off the balcony of the second-story bedroom, and that Mayer and Thalberg prevented her. Possibly it was precisely the outburst of emotion she needed, because after that she was ready to talk to the police.

The police, of course, had found out where Jean was staying. Several detectives, headed by Chief of Detectives Joe Taylor, soon appeared at the Bello home.

Jean was clad in a bathrobe. Her beautiful face showed the strain of her ordeal. Her eyes were sunken, her cheeks drawn. The heavy sedation she'd taken after receiving the news of her husband's death was working on her now, and her speech was slow.

"I simply can't understand it," she said. "I don't . . . I just don't know why he did it."

"What did he mean by that note?" asked Chief Taylor.

"I don't know," the actress replied. "I cannot by the wildest stretch of the imagination imagine what Paul meant in that note he left."

"Did he ever talk of suicide to you?" the detective chief asked.

"He has often talked of suicide," Harlow said, "but never with himself in mind, that I know of. More from a psychological interest than anything else, I would say. I can think of no reason why he should have felt it necessary to do this thing to himself.

"In one of these discussions about suicide he told me that his own mother had taken her life because she did not receive a cablegram from him on a certain day when she expected it. So there has been another suicide in the family."

A maid brought some tea in to the actress, and the detective waited until she drank some before he started questioning her again.

"Can you tell us," he finally began, "what

Mr. Bern did in the days leading up to his death?"

"Yes," said Harlow. "Friday night we dined at the home of Willis Goldbeck. Saturday we both were at the studio. As we left, he suggested that I go to my mother's house to spend the night, as I had to be back at the studio Sunday morning."

"Did you go?"

"Yes, I spent the night here at my mother's."

"What about Sunday?" Chief Taylor asked.

"Sunday evening, after work, I drove back to our home. We had a light snack, since no dinner had been ordered."

"Did your husband seem all right then?" the detective inquired.

"Well," said Harlow, "he complained of a bad headache, but he said it was because he'd been reading scripts all day. But he didn't seem overly depressed."

"Were you with him the whole night?"

"No," Harlow answered. "My stepfather had gone fishing over the weekend, and Paul suggested I go over to my mother's because she'd probably be lonesome. He said he'd meet me there later that night."

"Did he?" Detective Chief Taylor asked.

Harlow bowed her head and twisted her hands.

"No," she said softly. "That's the last I heard from him. Then . . . then I got the terrible news."

Harlow remained in bed in her mother's home, and the detectives left. It appeared to be a clear case of suicide, but under the law a coroner's inquest is required in any violent or extraordinary death. The inquest into Paul Bern's suicide was scheduled for September 9. In the meantime, the authorities were gathering other information in the case.

Bern's chauffeur confirmed some of Bern's activities shortly before his death. The chauffeur, Harold A. Garrison, told police that he'd picked up his employer at the M-G-M studio barbershop about 6 P.M. the previous Saturday. "When we got to the house, he told me to come back Sunday morning about 9. I came, as he said, and Carmichael (the butler) told me that Mr. Bern was still asleep. I hung around and waited until 4 o'clock, and then Carmichael went upstairs and came down to tell me that Mr. Bern was still asleep and that he couldn't get any sense out of him except that he wanted me to come back Monday morning." (It was on Monday morning that

105

Bern was found dead.)

Garrison also volunteered the information that Bern's gun, a pistol he usually kept in the glove compartment, wasn't in the car Saturday. The chauffeur had mentioned its absence to Bern, and Bern had replied: "Yes, I didn't bring it with me tonight."

Garrison pointed out to the police that Bern had been carrying a weapon in recent months because he'd almost been robbed by stickup men in the car.

But what seemed to emerge more and more as the authorities questioned friends and colleagues of the tormented Bern was his preoccupation with suicide in the months before his death.

One of his closest friends, John Gilbert, sorrowfully told police, "The circumstances surrounding the incident are too delicate and too close to my heart for me to discuss them now. But it was at a time when Bern was deeply hurt, and only then, that he would turn his thoughts to suicide. He was extremely sensitive. He would brood for days over some imagined slight.

"The ordinary pleasures of life meant little to him. He had become philosophical in his thoughts on death and eternity. He said to me once, 'My only reason for living is the opportunity to give others happiness. Should the time ever come when I believe I am no longer able to do that, I will not hesitate to snuff out the candle.'

"Paul Bern was my best friend. And if he thought that this was the time for him to go, it is not for me to criticize him."

Like Gilbert, David Selznick, another associate of Bern's, told of Bern's morbidity about suicide.

"He often discussed suicide in a philosophical vein," Selznick stated. "He said a man should be ready to die by his own hand when he had outlived his usefulness."

Louis B. Mayer also spoke of Bern's preoccupation with suicide, and so did Jean's stepfather, Marino Bello.

"I was told as recently as three weeks ago," he said on the eve of the inquest, "that Bern had said that he did not expect to live out the normal span of life, but would end it all."

As in every police inquiry, all sorts of rumors gain currency. One of them had been that Jean and Paul had quarreled violently the night before he shot himself to death.

"That's absolutely not so," Harlow countered. "There were no bad feelings between us."

One report was that the alleged argument came about because Jean wanted to sell their sumptuous home and buy another, deeding it to her mother and Bello.

But Bello scoffed at the reports. "It is untrue that Paul and Jean quarreled over deeding a house to Mrs. Bello and myself," he told police. "Why, I have more than Paul had, so what would be the reason?" Then Bello volunteered: "And neither is there anything to the story that Paul was helping me with financing a goldmine. For several years I have been operating mines as a stockholder."

Asked about the note Bern left, Bello gave this opinion: "He was apologizing to Jean for his suicide. If you marry a girl and soon afterward kill yourself, that is something to apologize for."

One of the witnesses Detective Chief Taylor talked to, who made it all but certain Bern was contemplating suicide, was Lawrence Stallings, the playwright.

"One day I saw Paul take a gun from his car and put it in his coat pocket," Stallings declared. "I said, 'What are you carrying a gun for?' and he replied: "I often think of suicide, and when the right mood and right moment come, I want to be ready."

While additional testimony came from friends of Bern's, telling of his apparent "suicide complex," evidence was accumulating to indicate that despondency over his own physical condition was responsible for the suicide.

Louis B. Mayer reported to the authorities that he had received a telephone call from Bern's personal physician, Dr. E. B. Jones, who was then in Honolulu vacationing. Mayer said Dr. Jones, who had known Bern well for the previous six years, had said he understood the motive and that he would leave Hawaii at once for California "where I shall be glad to give whatever information I have to the proper authorities."

On his arrival in Hollywood, Dr. Jones told police that "acute melancholia caused the suicide of Paul Bern. His act was personal and could involve no other person."

He promised to supply the clinical record of Bern to Coroner Frank Nance.

"This will be confidential information to the coroner," Dr. Jones told the pressmen later. "It is privileged information. I am sure this will clear up the case and show as impossible the theory that any other person was involved in Bern's death. Bern suffered from trivial things which became exaggerated in his mind and resulted in acute melancholia. I know that his act was a personal one. I think I can prove this to everyone's satisfaction."

The "theory that any other person was involved" to which Dr. Jones referred grew primarily out of one curious piece of testimony that was never explained. The head housekeeper told authorities that on Sunday night —the night before Bern's body was found— she heard a car pull out of the Bern driveway and roar off down the road at excessive speed. In a case involving such famous people, such a report is bound to mushroom into a fast-spreading rumor. It did, in fact, touch off some wild speculation that Bern was murdered. But nothing in the police investigation gave the rumor any support.

In time the inquest was held, and the official police ruling that came out of it was that Bern's death was suicide, brought on by melancholia that apparently evolved from depression and overwork.

Jean Harlow did not testify. Coroner Nance did not insist on it, and Jean's own personal physician had stated beforehand, "She is in no condition to be moved (from her mother's home) and it will be absolutely impossible for her to testify."

And so all investigation into Paul Bern's death ceased, but the inquiry did bring out one curious and heretofore undisclosed bit of information.

Even while he was married, Paul Bern was paying all the living expenses for another woman.

It's true that some of Bern's closest intimates had known of a rather loose association he'd had years earlier with another woman—a woman with whom he'd lived for a while and then, presumably, drifted away from. Now and then, it was assumed, he sent her some money, and perhaps helped her out in other ways. In time, nothing more was ever heard of her. Bern himself never mentioned her.

But the disclosures that came in the wake of Bern's death indicated that his relationship with the woman was of a wholly different nature. It hadn't been an idle, casual friendship at all. The evidence pointed to the fact that Bern had a deep sense of responsibility toward her, and never completely forsook her.

The public became aware of her existence two or three days after Bern's death, when his will came up for probate. The disclosure first came from George C. Clarkson, a Los

Angeles insurance man and a friend of Bern's. He said he knew of a will Bern had prepared years earlier in which his beneficiary was a woman named Dorothy Millette, whom Bern had met in the Academy of Dramatic Arts in 1911, just before his graduation and just after her entry into the school. The will naming Miss Millette as beneficiary was in the offices of Henry Utall, at 521 Fifth Avenue in New York City. Utall confirmed the existence of the will and would have filed it in probate, except that other attorneys for Paul Bern hastily produced a later will leaving the bulk of his estate to Jean Harlow.

The emergence of Dorothy Millette from Bern's past touched off a spasm of poolside talk and rumor about the slain executive's "phantom wife." Then piece by piece, fragments of information began falling into place, forming a picture of the association Bern had with the woman.

Twenty-one years earlier, in 1911, Bern was just completing his two-year course at the Academy of Dramatic Arts in Carnegie Hall, New York. There he was introduced by a mutual friend to a young and "strikingly beautiful" blonde girl, Dorothy Millette. At the time, she was aspiring to become a great stage actress.

The introduction was made by Joseph Graham, the stage director, and it apparently led to a romance. It was said that Bern and Miss Millette had actually planned on getting married at one time. They didn't, but they nevertheless began living together in an apartment in Jersey City. They stayed there for a couple of years and then moved into New York's Hotel Algonquin as "Mr. and Mrs. Paul Bern."

It was about this time that Bern was hired for one of the supporting roles in *Too Many Cooks*, with Frank Craven as the lead. Miss Millette had a smaller part in the same play. It was the only known time the two appeared in any production together. Thereafter Dorothy Millette apparently faded from the theatrical scene, although she continued to live with Bern, and Bern continued to introduce her to people as his wife.

In the early years of their life together, the two had financial troubles, as do many young people seeking a career in the theater. Their money troubles might have been the cause of their separation. At any rate, some time in 1921 or 1922, after ten years or more together, they split up. Dorothy Millette continued living in the Algonquin as "Mrs. Paul Bern," but Bern himself went out to the West Coast, where he began prospering, shortly thereafter, in the movies.

With Bern out of her life, Miss Millette took to brooding almost constantly, friends said. But she never went to the doctor, because of her religion. She was a Christian Scientist. Little became known of her as the years moved on. In time, presumably, nobody made the connection any longer between the fast-rising Paul Bern in Hollywood and the retiring, silent "Mrs. Paul Bern" at the Algonquin in New York, a continent away. By the time Bern married Jean Harlow, there was a vague understanding among the people who had known of Bern's association with Miss Millette in the past that she was now in some mental institution.

But she wasn't. She reappeared in Hollywood about the time Bern married Harlow. She abruptly checked out of the Algonquin one day and told the desk clerk simply, "I am going to Los Angeles to straighten out some financial matters."

She dropped from sight for the next several weeks, but her name again exploded into prominence when, just two days after Bern killed himself, a San Francisco hotel announced that it had recently received a check signed by Bern, and made payable to a "Miss D. Millette." So it was clear that Dorothy Millette was in San Francisco on the day that Bern fatally shot himself.

As the story of the Bern-Millette relationship came into sharper focus, it became known that all of Miss Millette's bills at the Algonquin had been paid over the years, first by Paul Bern himself and later by his brother, Henry.

Frank Case, then manager of the Algonquin, reported that Paul Bern made it his habit to visit Dorothy Millette whenever he came East —usually about twice a year.

Further information came from George C. Clarkson, the insurance man. He said that life insurance policies held by Bern were payable to a trust fund handled by a New York bank, for the benefit of Dorothy Millette. Bern kept a large sum of money with the New York Trust Company for Miss Millette's support and for payments of the life insurance policies, Clarkson said. The amount Bern paid Miss Millette was never publicly stated, but one close friend of Bern's said it amounted to some $200 a week.

When the existence of Dorothy Millette

became known to the public after Bern's death, reporters asked the distraught Jean Harlow if she had ever heard of the "Phantom Mate."

"I knew he was paying some medical bills for her," Miss Harlow said. "Paul really never talked about it, and I wasn't interested."

But Harlow's father, the pugnacious Marino Bello, snapped, when asked the same thing: "We knew nothing of Bern's past life. If I had known of it before Bern married Jean, the wedding would have taken place over my dead body."

There are two postscripts to the Dorothy Millette episode. The first is tragic. Three months after Bern killed himself, Miss Millette, in a fit of depression, threw herself into the Sacramento River one dark night and drowned. She left no note, nothing to tell of the deep feeling she must have had for the man who sustained her in a strange, in many ways unbelievable, relationship through all those years.

The second postscript took several years to complete. It was a court fight, instituted by relatives of Dorothy Millette who were seeking part of Bern's estate on the grounds that he and Miss Millette had lived "in a state of matrimony" during their early years together, and for the further reason that Bern had been her benefactor, paying all bills and living expenses, for more than ten years after they separated.

The court fight was started by a sister of Dorothy's, Viona Millette, and the estate of another sister, Mrs. John Hartranft. In the end—the case was finally settled in April 1936 —the sisters were awarded $2,000 from the $48,000 estate left by Bern to Jean Harlow.

Chapter Five

In the immediate aftermath of Paul Bern's death, the grieving Jean Harlow went into seclusion. She saw few people outside her immediate family. But the public's demands on her were great, and pressure began building almost immediately for her to return to work. *Red-Headed Woman* had been a smash hit and permanently solidified her into the type that ultimately made her screen reputation, that of the frankly unabashed and humorously imprudent woman of the world. Now both her studio and the public were clamoring for more.

After a couple of months of idleness following Bern's death, Harlow emerged from her shell and moved cautiously back into the high-tempoed swing of Hollywood and the movies. The work helped. Harlow was naturally an outgoing person, someone who delighted in having people around her. Before long, the scars of Paul Bern's death seemed to vanish, and the old Harlow was back in harness, turning out *Red Dust*—another picture co-starring Clark Gable—*Hold Your Man*, *Dinner at Eight*, and *Blonde Bombshell*.

The resumption of life stimulated her. She began seeing other men, having casual dates, traveling. But most of all she threw herself into her work. She had become a true professional, a woman who knew and understood the meaning of movies and the role the "star" must play. She knew she belonged to the 70 million fans who spent an hour or two each week with her and with her brother and sister stars. Once, on the set of a movie she was making, she told writer Douglas Churchill:

"When I left the church after Paul's funeral, people broke through the police lines and surged about me. There were words of sympathy and ghastly words and demands for autographs. I was shocked. They seemed too heartless. Later, as I thought about it, a realization came. They meant no disrespect. They were kindly and gracious and thoughtful in their own lives, and had I been an individual they would have treated me as one of their own. But to them I was not a person. I was an institution. I had no more personality than a corporation."

Another time, she admitted candidly:

"I'm lucky and I know it. I'm not a great actress and except for the early part of my life in Hollywood I never thought that I was. But I happen to have something the public likes. I am fortunate because I am able to appreciate this.

"I think I know the people who go to see me on the screen. Some actresses outgrow their public. They speak of the morons. But ever since I clicked, I have worked with but one realization, that in me, whether I could define it or not, was something that the public wanted."

And want her they did.

By now, her fan mail had shot up to 5,000 letters a week, and M-G-M had signed her to a seven-year contract. Her salary went up to $40,000 a week, placing her near the pinnacle of top money-makers in Hollywood.

Her career was soaring. The public adored her, the press pampered her wherever she went. That phenomenon of Hollywood had happened. Chemistry and mechanics had transmuted flesh and blood into a vital force. A calcium light projected through a strip composed of gum cotton, camphor and silver salts, accompanied by electric vibrations from a sound track, had converted a personality into an institution that served as a common denominator in conversation from Times Square to the smallest village in Arizona.

And Harlow, now that the pain of Paul Bern's suicide had been eased by the healing powers of time and hard work, reveled in it.

And now, too, she was finding herself able to bring some order into her personal life. She was becoming organized. Her workday was long, usually starting at eight in the morning and ending at six or seven in the evening. Then she would usually go to her home, eat a quiet dinner alone or with her mother and stepfather or perhaps one or two close friends, and then retire to bed early. While Harlow had dates with a dazzling parade of men, she apparently took none of them seriously.

Until she married one of them.

His name was Hal Rossen, and their wedding, in September 1933, just a year after Paul Bern killed himself, took Hollywood completely by surprise.

Actually, they'd been friends for a long time. Hal, a short, quiet man of thirty-eight, was one of the really great cameramen in motion pictures. His services were sought by all the major studios. He had been the chief cameraman on *Red-Headed Woman*, and even then, Harlow, who knew virtually nothing about the mechanics of her craft, was struck by Rossen's ability. He worked with her again in *Red Dust*—the first picture she did after Bern's death—and he was frequently at her side, lending her solace, comforting her.

Because he was a good friend, and because he was probably the top cameraman in Hollywood, Harlow soon began requesting that Rossen do all of her pictures. They worked well together. She listened attentively to his suggestions—where to stand, which way to face, how to pose. All the technical tricks that helped bring her so forcefully to life on the screen. And more and more, when the day's shooting was over, it would be Hal Rossen that she invited home to dinner, or would accompany to a restaurant.

The stage was set for their marriage during the shooting of *Blonde Bombshell*, a bombastic satire of Hollywood life co-starring Lee Tracy. Hal Rossen was the cameraman. When the production was completed and *Bombshell* was launched, the whole cast took off for a few days' vacation in the cactus country of Arizona.

While there, Harlow and Rossen slipped away together to Yuma and eloped.

Jean, looking back on the romance later, recalled: "When I first fell in love with him I don't know. Perhaps it was during the filming of *Red Dust*. Of all the eyes on me at that time, I seemed to feel his were the kindliest. I rather felt he was in love with me. We saw a great deal of each other while we were shooting that picture, and during later productions, and all of a sudden I knew the overwhelming truth: I was in love with him. He was my man."

Hal himself said he'd had his eye on Jean for a long time. "For years I admired her," he said. "From the very moment my cameras starting clicking with Jean in front of them, I was in love. I had eyes for no one else. At first I hardly dared hope. Then I saw that she —well, she rather liked me. You know the rest."

Jean was so delighted with her new role as Mrs. Rossen that she wrote at the time: "I love him so much I don't even care when he beats me at golf. And that just about tells it all, doesn't it? If you care that much about a man, of course you want to marry him. At least any golf addict will realize that.

"My romance with Hal began, like many another romance, on the job. He had been my cameraman for several pictures at M-G-M. I remember seeing the first 'takes' of *Red-Headed Woman* and realizing I was in the hands of a wonderful photographer. You know, a photographer can almost make or break a girl in pictures if he has a mind to, and to realize I was in the hands of one who I could be confident would do his best by me was a grand and glorious feeling.

"And that confidence in Hal as a photographer grew and extended to other things until now I am as confident in him as a husband as I am that he is the best cameraman in the world.

"Our first real 'date,' however, was for a game of golf. My stepfather, Marino Bello, had wanted me to take up the game for a long time and finally he contrived a threesome consisted of Hal, himself and me. He and Hal were old friends, by the way.

"I remember I was pretty terrible, but that particular occasion I number as one of the red-letter days in my life because I was so happy. I realized then that here was a man who would make a wonderful friend. A man who was interesting, considerate, charming. And this feeling of appreciation grew as time went on.

"And so it was natural that we should fall in love, I think. To me, love has always meant friendship, understanding, mutual tastes. And, moreover, our work brought us closer together.

"I am asked just when we became engaged. But I can't answer that. We have never been exactly 'engaged.' However, I can describe the moment when we decided to get married. We were on location in Arizona shooting *Blonde Bombshell*. One night, after we had finished shooting, Hal and I went for a walk.

"We stopped beneath a giant saguaro, silvered in the pale desert moonlight. Everything was perfect. The picture was going well. God seemed in his heaven—a heaven white with stars, as you'll remember if you've ever seen the desert sky at night—and all seemed, indeed, right with the world. Hal looked at me. I looked at him. He said, 'Let's get married.' And I said, 'All right.'

"That was on a Saturday night. We went back. The next night, the four of us—my mother, my stepfather, Hal and I—were sitting around discussing plans for the wedding. Suddenly I knew that the time had come. We promptly arranged for a plane, and we went to Yuma.

"I believe that I have reached the point where I know what I want. And I wanted Hal. He is, I think, the most sincere, the finest, kindest, most honorable man I have ever known."

Harlow was then twenty-two—sixteen years younger than Hal Rossen. But the age difference didn't bother her.

"I am sure the difference in our years will not matter," she said. "I always have known people older than myself. Besides, Hal and I like the same things—another reason for our love. We play together like a couple of kids. He is just old enough to be my mentor. I respect him so I'll always heed his advice. He has been very kind to me; now it is up to me to repay his kindness. I can and will do so. I consider him the ideal husband, lover, golf partner and cameraman.

"Oh, I just know that ours will be one Hollywood marriage that lasts. This is just the beginning of my new life as Mrs. Harold G. Rossen."

Once they were married, Rossen moved his things into Jean's house and they settled down to quiet living. Jean had never liked the frantic nightlife of Hollywood, and Hal, a retiring, mild-mannered man, loathed it. So marriage for them fell into a routine of hard work for a long day, then home for an uneventful evening. The weekends were spent at golf, swimming in their pool, and some occasional light entertaining.

On the surface, the marriage seemed to be going smoothly. But Jean's friends wondered. Hal Rossen was in a number of ways quite similar to Paul Bern. Like Bern, he was shy, introverted, quiet. He, too, was frail, and he had a remarkable physical resemblance to Bern. Did Jean enter her marriage with Hal in a search for kindness, for peace, for safety? Could the glittering movie queen really be in love with a man who seemed to be the antithesis of everything she was and stood for?

And so Hollywood wondered, and waited.

They didn't have long to wait. The first rumblings of discontent began to be heard from the big Harlow house in Beverly Hills that Christmas—a scant three months after they were married. No one knew quite what the trouble was, but Jean spent part of the holidays at her parents' home. Afterward, Jean and Hal seemed to grow distant toward one another. They barely talked to each other on the movie sets. They did no entertaining together. The California winter came and went and by March, although no formal announcement had been made, everyone knew the Rossens were through. Two months later it was official.

On May 26, 1934, seven months and eighteen days after the blonde bombshell and the ace cameraman married, Jean Harlow picked up the telephone and told a Hollywood gossip columnist:

"Hal and I have separated, and I am going to seek a divorce. Our marriage is all over. But I want to say that Hal is a splendid man, and I regret more than I can say that our marriage has been a failure. We simply were not meant for each other. There is no other man or woman. And I won't say it's Hal's fault any more than it's mine."

Hal Rossen had packed his belongings and retreated to a different, safer world, a world devoid of the most glamorous girl on earth. The doomsayers had been right. Nearly a year later, on March 12, 1935, the beautiful actress entered Judge Elliott Craig's court in Los

Angeles and walked out eight minutes later a free woman. She had obtained an interlocutory divorce decree from Rossen, who by then had moved to London to pursue movie camerawork there.

Harlow was accompanied into the courtroom by her mother and her attorney, Oscar A. Trippet. Jean was wearing a long brown sable coat. On the stand in the crowded courtroom, the glamorous movie queen was asked to "give some details" about the mental cruelty she was charging against Rossen. Jean testified:

"At a party in our honor, a young man sang a song by request. Mr. Rossen was terribly sarcastic and embarrassed me greatly. He was jealous of my friends, of my time and of my position—of everything I had. This affected my health and world."

She told the court that a property settlement had been worked out already, and then submitted to further questioning by her lawyer.

Q. Did your husband's conduct cause you to be nervous and unfitted to carry on your work at the studio?

A. Yes. Whenever I had guests he was so rude and insulted them so that I finally refused to ask them to come to the house.

Q. Did he refuse to attend a wedding at which you were matron of honor?

A. Yes.

Q. In what other ways did he embarrass you?

A. Within twelve hours after the wedding, he became very irritable. He was jealous of me and of my work. He never missed an opportunity to belittle me and my profession."

Jean's mother, Mrs. Marino Bello, was called to the witness stand as a corroborative witness.

"There was a very evident intention on his part to belittle Jean," Mrs. Bello said.

Mrs. Bello elaborated on the testimony of her daughter relative to the incident when the man was singing at the party.

"In the middle of the song," said Mrs. Bello, "Mr. Rossen, who was standing at the head of the stairway, spoke up and said, "That will do. That is sufficient."

Jean's attorney asked her mother, "Did you notice if your daughter became nervous and irritated, and if so, what caused it?"

Mrs. Bello replied: "Yes. It was because we never knew what Mr. Rossen's attitude was going to be. Sometimes he would come home and be very affable and cheerful, and at other times he would be entirely different."

When the eight minutes were over, Jean Harlow's third marriage lay in shambles. She had her divorce from Rossen. It had been Rossen's second attempt; his first marriage to Nina Byron, a one-time Follies girl, had ended in divorce in 1927 after two stormy years.

As for Harlow, when the session was over and she strode down the courthouse steps, a horde of reporters was waiting.

One of them asked, "Do you think you'll ever marry again?"

Harlow fixed him with a stony glare and snapped, "No more marriages."

Chapter Six

But she was only twenty-four, and highly volatile, and of course beautiful, and no one really took her seriously.

In the meantime, it was back to work for Harlow—furious work, just as she'd done following the death of Paul Bern. Her career was reaching its zenith. She did *Girl From Missouri*, *Reckless*, *China Seas* and *Riffraff*. At one time, four different movies of hers were being shown in theaters across the country. She was "hot property," perhaps the top box-office attraction of the day. The public was clamoring for her more than ever. At the smallest excuse, newspapers would splash her name in headlines. They would grab at anything. Once, Jean was badly sunburned and decided to enter a hospital for a day. It made page one news everywhere.

She had lunch two or three times with book publisher Donald Friede. Suddenly she was "romantically linked" to him in every important gossip column in the land. An attack of appendicitis she had once was enough to make the papers put out an extra. And Harlow loved every minute of it. Once she told an interviewer she was changing the color of her hair from platinum blonde to a soft brown— "brownette" she called it—and wondered aloud if her fans would approve. Within a week, she received 15,000 letters, the overwhelming majority of them saying it was fine with them.

Jean Harlow was by now a beloved figure. All her millions of fans somehow felt a personal, intimate relationship with her. She was their property. She belonged to them. Her male counterpart was probably Clark Gable, the big guy with the boyish grin. There was a little bit of Gable in the minds and hearts of every man watching him on the screen; and so it was with Harlow. The women empathized with her, and at the same time idealized her. The men, of course, were crazy about her. And she was now firmly at the top of her craft, a true artisan, a girl who might not be the best actress in the world, but one who knew her way around Hollywood and motion pictures—a hard-working, dependable craftsman with a world of experience behind her.

It was about this time that Ann Marsters, a writer, recorded a friendly and warm conversation Harlow had one day with Clark Gable. It was an easy, relaxed conversation, some unimportant chatter between two old and good friends who had known each other since the first critical stages of their careers. Now they were reminiscing.

"Do you remember," Jean began, "the first time we met each other?"

"Sure," Gable answered promptly. "It was six years ago on the set of *The Secret Six*. Wallace Beery introduced us and told us not to be nervous. I was playing the part of a newspaper reporter and you were a gangster's moll."

"They weren't very large parts," said Jean. "And I remember that we spent most of our time watching Wallace Beery when he was before the camera. I had an idea that if I watched him closely enough I could learn all the tricks of acting."

Gable smiled. "I can see that it didn't do you

the slightest bit of good. Somehow your acting just doesn't remind me of Wallace Beery."

The year before they met in *The Secret Six*, Gable had appeared in *The Painted Desert* and Harlow had made *Hell's Angels*.

Gable continued ruminating: "They both did a lot for us, but even so, there followed a period of uncertainty for both of us, and at the time of our meeting we were both wandering around in a fog. I didn't know what was ahead of me—but I had a feeling that Jean would make good." He looked at Harlow, and she smiled. Gable continued:

"My first impression of Jean was of a girl with a glittering kind of beauty. She has what I call a radiant quality, as though she were always standing in the sunlight."

Jean interrupted. "Don't mind me," she said dryly. "Do go on, and I'll just pretend I'm not here. But can it be you're confusing me with my dress?" She was referring to the dress she was then wearing, a sparkling, beaded creation. Every time she moved it seemed to send out sharp little darts of silver. With her platinum hair, she did indeed seem to be standing in the golden sunlight.

"Anyway," Gable resumed, "we were first starred together about a year after our modest appearances in *The Secret Six*. The picture was *Red Dust*, and it really gave us the big break we were looking for. After that, we co-starred in an average of one picture a year. There was *Hold Your Man*, *China Seas*, and *Wife Versus Secretary*.

"I think Jean brought me good luck, because everything went so smoothly after we met. Up until then I had worked like a dog to get some sort of recognition in this town."

"I always told you you'd get it some day," said Jean. "And I didn't say it just to encourage you. I really believed it. I think you're a lot handsomer now than you were back in those early days." She winked at him playfully. "You were a little lanky then, and a bit bashful."

"Oh, so that's what you thought of me, is it?" Gable laughed.

"I thought you were very nice," Jean replied. "And outside of your looks, you haven't changed at all."

Jean went on, almost as though Gable weren't there. "Clark is a splendid friend for anyone to have," she said. "He seems to make your troubles his troubles, and your triumphs his triumphs. I know that no one ever worked harder than Clark for success. But at the same time, he was, and is, always ready to give someone else a helping hand.

"He's such a sensible, cheerful person. He seems to be able to turn dark clouds into bright ones quicker than anyone I've ever known. And he can do it without any fuss or dramatics. When we work in pictures together it always improves my disposition about fifty percent."

In Gable's view, Harlow had great potentiality for becoming an important dramatic actress as well as a fine comedienne.

"I really think you'd make another Garbo," he said to Jean. "Some of your touches, even in your whackiest roles, show a lot of talent for drama. I see the same thing in Carole, too. Why don't you take a crack at it?"

"Maybe I will," Jean said, "but I'd want you as my co-star."

They were destined to star together again, in *Saratoga*, but it was a picture marred by tragedy. It was while Jean was filming *Saratoga* that she became ill and died.

Gable's mention of "Carole" referred to Carole Lombard, another bright, young, and beautiful Hollywood star. At the time of his conversation with Harlow, Gable had been seeing a lot of Carole, and rumors were flying fast that one day soon the two would be married.

In a way, it was ironical that Gable and Harlow had become such true and fast friends, because the next—and the most important—romantic interlude in her life was William Powell, the suave leading man and star of *The Thin Man* series, whose latest marriage had ended on the rocks—his marriage to Carole Lombard.

Powell and Miss Lombard were divorced in Nevada, in August 1933. Thus he was free when Jean's separation from Hal Rossen was announced. In a short time, Powell and Harlow, who had met while making a movie together, began to see each other constantly. And for the first time Harlow's friends saw some chance for happiness for her in marriage. Powell, though several years older than the vibrant blonde actress, seemed much more attuned to her personality than her first three husbands had been. He was wealthy, famous, a star as big as Jean herself, and not likely to be cowed by her great popularity and eminence in the motion picture industry.

Before long, Jean's "friendship"—that's how she always referred to it—with Powell became the talk of Hollywood, and the big question on everyone's lips was, "when will they get married?"

Despite Jean's apparently casual reference to Powell as simply "a friend," when she discussed him in public, she made it abundantly clear to her intimates that she desperately wanted Bill for her fourth husband.

At one point she cried to Adela Rogers St. John, her dear friend: "He won't marry me. He loves me, but he says he's had one beautiful, young blonde wife and he's approaching middle age—he's very witty about it—he wants to put on his slippers and stay home nights instead of chasing the blonde bombshell around night clubs trying to fend off half the men in the world. You know I loathe night clubs. He won't believe me when I say I only want him and a home. He kisses me and laughs and says we'd never make a go of it. Do you think he's remembering Paul?"

Miss St. John said that she wasn't sure, but wasn't it ironic that Carole Lombard, who'd been Bill's beautiful, young, blonde wife, should have cost Jean her chance at happiness, when Carole herself was so happy with Clark Gable? Later Miss St. John told friends that she felt she couldn't interfere because, after all, Powell was a wise, intelligent, experienced man of the world, and he surely knew Jean very well.

Jean, who had a strong friendship with Clark Gable, told him: "I have never known anyone like Bill. Just being with him is happiness enough for me. We spend the days together golfing, riding, motoring; anything as long as we do it together. It's perfect. The vacation we took to Yosemite National Park was one of the happiest times of my life. It isn't that we do anything extraordinary, but just the closeness we feel toward each other. Bill understands me and accepts me. He doesn't try to change me. I've had three bad marriages and I wouldn't even consider a fourth unless I was absolutely certain. Not just of the man, but of whether I was ready, mature enough. I don't want to make any more mistakes with my life. I'm tired of being a 'blonde bombshell.' I want to relax and live quietly with a man I can love completely. I know I can have the life I want with Bill."

As for Bill, the suave actor whose portrayals of the dashing, clever detective, Nick Carter, had skyrocketed him into Hollywood's loftiest echelons, in terms of both money and fame, was obviously in love with Harlow. But he assumed a publicly bemused attitude to conceal what was probably an acutely sensitive matter to him.

When asked if he would marry the platinum-haired beauty, his stock answer was: "I'm too old and tired for child brides. Delightful and lovely as she is, Jean needs a nice young man who can keep up with her, not a dull pipe-and-slipper type."

After sixteen years of hard work, Bill Powell had hit the top, one of the highest paid actors in the world, able to earn $450,000 during a year which still left him seven months free. For *The Baroness and the Butler* he was paid $40,000 a week for six weeks' work, topping the record of Constance Bennett, who received $30,000 a week over a period in 1932-33.

He worked hard and worried a lot. He worried when the talkies came. But he did more than survive them. This boy who started out with a harsh prairie twang had improved his voice so much that his diction was held up as a model to young Americans aspiring to screen careers.

At one time, almost as a lark, Powell had a house built for himself in Beverly Hills. It was the sort of house that only a crazy set designer of movie epics could have concocted. Tourist agencies ran bus trips to see "Powell's Folly."

When he drove his car up, a photoelectric cell opened the gates and floodlit the drive. The garage doors swung open.

He could press a button in his bedroom for a wall to swing back and reveal a gymnasium. A turn of a lever brought beer up through a pipe from the basement. His library boasted a rare collection of first editions—of very dull literature. It was his pride to find a book so dull that even reading the title would lull him to sleep.

But the Powell sense of humor survived even this whimsical extravagance. "I was never comfortable in the darn place," he said. "It was so comfortable that I felt uncomfortable."

He sold it in 1936.

No Hollywood producer had ever had a quicker eye for feminine beauty than Bill Powell's. He once said that he had been "girl conscious" from the age of fourteen, when he took his first girl friend to the five-cent seats at the local cinema. Later he saved up to go to drama school and then spent the money on girl friends.

His charming gallantry on the screen became part of him early in life. Somebody once asked him, in his poor days, why he gave waitresses such generous tips. "I like to see their eyes shine," he said.

When asked about marriage, he said: "I believe there is something in my nature which prevents my making a successful marriage. It may be my fault or it may be Hollywood's, but my marriages seem to be fated."

After the tragic blow fell, and Jean Harlow was dead, in a particularly revealing moment he confided to a close friend: "I never seem able to catch up with happiness."

In spite of Powell's reluctance to take the giant step of marriage, most of his and Jean's friends believed that someday soon he would; that it was just a matter of time. He couldn't know, nor could the world, that fate would step in and cruelly rob him of that precious commodity, time.

At the very height of their romance, and at the summit of her own career, illness swept over Jean Harlow and snuffed out her young, full life.

Actually, the illness that was to bring her death on June 7, 1937, had begun the previous February, when she contracted a slight case of influenza while returning from a trip to New York. She was treated for it at the time, and the condition seemed to clear up, but it flared again in April when Jean had two wisdom teeth removed. Thereafter her health remained frail as she continued on her hectic schedule of personal appearances and long hard hours of work before the camera.

The critical attack came while she was on the set of *Saratoga*, the picture she was currently making with Clark Gable. She was running through a scene when suddenly she grew weak and had to sit down. She looked up at Gable and said with a wan smile, "I . . . I don't know what it is, Clark, I don't feel very well. Maybe I'd better go and lie down."

She went in and rested on a couch in her dressing room. Five minutes later the studio doctor, who had been summoned by Gable, stepped through the door and examined her. She told him of the recent attacks of influenza. The physician examined her thoroughly, then had her removed to her home in a chauffeured limousine. At home, a corps of nurses attended her 24 hours a day. The attack hit her on May 29. By June 3 she had rallied enough so that some of the nurses were relieved of duty. Others stayed on, and Jean's mother was at her bedside literally day and night. The following night Harlow's condition deteriorated, and she was rushed to Good Samaritan Hospital in Hollywood. For two days her condition fluctuated. Her personal physician, Dr. E. C. Fishbaugh, attended her constantly. She rallied once again valiantly, but the tragedy that had dogged her through so much of her life now closed in on her personally, and at 11:37 in the morning of June 7, Jean Harlow died.

She drew her last breath and sank back in death as firemen worked over her with an inhalator and Dr. Fishbaugh, another physician and two nurses worked desperately to save her life with all the aides known to medical science.

The death room was more dramatic than any cinematic setting the beautiful actress had ever graced. Her mother and stepfather were there, and so was William Powell—pale, near shock himself as he saw the life ebb away from the girl he loved so much and now knew he was going to lose.

On the bed, her face nearly as white as the sheets she lay on, Jean Harlow struggled for breath.

Three firemen stood over her, working the inhalator, trying desperately to increase her rapidly diminishing breathing. Dr. Fishbaugh and Dr. L. S. Chapman stood anxiously by, advising the firemen and the half dozen nurses in the room. The minutes ticked by as Jean's breathing came slower and slower.

Then suddenly the breathing stopped.

The firemen worked heroically trying to revive her. After several minutes they stopped. They looked at one another, then at the others in the room, and finally at the body of Jean Harlow. Then they stood up slowly, their faces wreathed in sorrow.

The two doctors stepped over to the bed and examined her. Then Dr. Fishbaugh shook his head solemnly and intoned, "She's gone."

Her mother turned to Marino Bello and buried her face in his shoulder. "Poor Jean, my poor little girl," she cried softly.

Powell, numb with shock, stepped over to the bed and gazed down on the lifeless figure. Then suddenly he collapsed into inconsolable tears and rushed from the room out into the corridor, where Warner Baxter, his closest friend, had been waiting. Powell ran to Baxter and cried, "Why, oh why must she die? It's terrible, terrible, Warner."

Baxter consoled Powell and led him to another room down the hall.

Jean's mother and stepfather remained in the death room another twenty minutes, then slowly walked out, the weight of their grief etched on their faces. Again Mrs. Bello buried her face in her husband's shoulder, and the two walked out of the hospital and to a waiting car.

Afterward, Dr. Fishbaugh came out and said, "Miss Harlow died of uremic poisoning. Every known method of eliminating the poison was being used. Dr. Chapman and I worked incessantly for hours on Miss Harlow."

He said the star had received two blood transfusions in the final hours. "Also," he added, "intravenous solutions were administered."

A hospital report subsequently stated that attempts had been made while the actress was still at home to persuade her to undergo an operation to relieve the acute uremic poisoning condition, but that the star refused because of her Christian Science faith. In the hospital, she again refused. The uremic poisoning spread to her brain, causing swelling known as cerebral edema. It was that which actually caused her death.

All of Hollywood went into mourning. As the mighty and the famous of the film colony prepared to pay homage to her, Louis B.

Mayer, head of M-G-M, ordered the studio closed on the day of the funeral.

The funeral itself, although private and closed to all but the film beauty's family and closest friends, drew thousands of curious spectators to the Wee Kirk O' the Heather in Forest Lawn Memorial Park in nearby Glendale. Extra police had to be called out to control the crowds.

A simple Christian Science service was offered, read by Mrs. Genevieve Smith, a Christian Science practitioner and reader, and a friend of Miss Harlow's for the last eight years of her life.

Nelson Eddy and Jeanette MacDonald sang "Indian Love Call" and "Ah Sweet Mystery of Life."

At the mortuary, her mother wept. "The world didn't understand my baby," she said. "Our friends knew she wasn't the type of person she was portrayed as on the screen. She never said an unkind word about anyone. She was always cheerful, always looked for the best in everyone."

But the most tragic figure of all was tall, erect William Powell. He stood next to Jean in mute grief at the mortuary while her shining hair was brushed for the last time before lace was laid over her in the glinting bronze casket. And only then did he speak, a soft private lament as the tears streamed down his eyes. "Jean . . . Jean. . . ."

A short while later, Jean Harlow was laid to rest, and then it was over. Almost immediately, a flood of condolences began pouring in to the family. The statements told eloquently of the great fondness everyone she'd worked with felt for her.

"She was a beautiful and gallant trouper," said Gary Cooper.

"The suddenness of her passing makes it the more terrible for those who knew her," said Bing Crosby.

From Eddie Cantor came this accolade: "Jean Harlow richly merited the esteem we all had for her, both as an actress and as a person. Her loss is a blow to all of us in pictures."

David Selznick praised her "gay spirit" and said "her good nature and generosity were unequaled."

"Jean Harlow," said Mary Pickford, "had a brilliant career. She lived a full and abundant life and in my belief will continue to do so, although invisible to our mortal eyes."

Still others came.

Cecil B. De Mille called her "one of the

most vital personalities to emerge on the screen in a decade."

Fred Astaire praised her as "a fine artist and one of Hollywood's most beloved citizens."

And Clark Gable, her old and good friend, could only say, when approached by a reporter, "I am too overcome by grief to make any comment."

And so the saga of Jean Harlow had come to an end. There were postscripts from time to time—when her mother died; when her will was probated and showed, surprisingly, that she'd left an estate of only $41,000 from the $1,000,000-plus she'd made as a movie queen; when, years later, Hollywood wanted to do a picture of Jean's life starring another tragic figure, Marilyn Monroe.

But these incidents were somehow distant and apart from the real-life figure of Jean Harlow. The blithe spirit that had captivated so many millions of people in her lifetime was gone and could never return. She would be preserved for centuries to come in her films and in the musty archives of ten thousand newspapers and libraries across the country, but the vibrancy, the spirit, the essence of the golden girl was no more on this earth. She would be missed and lamented in the aching hearts of the crushed William Powell, the good pal Clark Gable, the dear friends whose lives she illumined so brightly, and most of all in the sorrowing hearts of the 70 million who were there at the birth of the Blonde Bombshell, the only one of her kind, the incomparable Harlow.

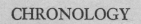

CHRONOLOGY

1929—"The Saturday Night Kid"
Paramount. Cast: Clara Bow, James Hall, Jean
Arthur, Edna May Oliver. Director: Edward
Sutherland.

1930—"Hell's Angels"
United Artists. Cast: Ben Lyon, James Hall,
John Darrow. Director: Howard Hughes.

1931—"Public Enemy"
Warner Bros. Cast: James Cagney, Beryl
Mercer, Donald Cook, Joan Blondell. Direc-
tor: William Wellman.

1931—"The Secret Six"
M-G-M. Cast: Wallace Beery, Lewis Stone,
John Mack Brown, Clark Gable, Ralph Bel-
lamy. Director: George Hill.

Chronology

1931—"The Iron Man"
Universal. Cast: Lew Ayres, Robert Armstrong. Director: Tod Browning.

1931—"Goldie"
Fox. Cast: Spencer Tracy. Director: Benjamin Stoloff.

1931—"The Platinum Blonde"
Columbia. Cast: Loretta Young, Reginald Owens. Director: Frank Capra.

1931—"Three Wise Girls"
Columbia. Cast: Mae Clarke, Marie Prevost, Andy Devine. Director: William Beaudine.

1932—"The Beast Of The City"
M-G-M. Cast: Walter Huston, Wallace Ford, Jean Hersholt. Director: Charles Brabin.

1932—"The Red Headed Woman"
M-G-M. Cast: Chester Morris, Lewis Stone, Una Merkel, May Robson, Charles Boyer. Director: Jack Conway.

1932—"Red Dust"
M-G-M. Cast: Clark Gable, Gene Raymond, Mary Astor. Director: Victor Fleming.

Chronology

1933—"Bombshell"
M-G-M. Cast: Lee Tracy, Franchot Tone, Pat O'Brien. Director: Victor Fleming.

1933—"Dinner At Eight"
M-G-M. Cast: Marie Dressler, John Barrymore, Wallace Beery, Lionel Barrymore, Lee Tracy, Billie Burke, Jean Hersholt, Madge Evans, May Robson. Director: George Cukor.

1933—"Hold Your Man"
M-G-M. Cast: Clark Gable, Muriel Kirkland. Director: Sam Wood.

1934—"The Girl From Missouri"
M-G-M. Cast: Lionel Barrymore, Franchot Tone, Lewis Stone, Patsy Kelly, Allan Mowbray, Nat Pendleton. Director: Jack Conway.

1935—"Reckless"
M-G-M. Cast: William Powell, Franchot Tone, May Robson, Rosalind Russell, Nina Mae McKinney. Director: David O. Selznick.

1935—"China Seas"
M-G-M. Cast: Clark Gable, Wallace Beery, Lewis Stone, Rosalind Russell, Dudley Digges, Robert Benchley, Akim Tamiroff. Director: Tay Garnett.

1936—"Riffraff"

M-G-M. Cast: Spencer Tracy, Una Merkel, Joseph Calleia, Mickey Rooney, George Givot, Victor Killian. Director: J. Walter Ruben.

1936—"Wife Versus Secretary"

M-G-M. Cast: Clark Gable, Myrna Loy, May Robson, James Stewart. Director: Clarence Brown.

1936—"Suzy"

M-G-M. Cast: Franchot Tone, Cary Grant, Lewis Stone, Benita Hume, Reginald Mason, Una O'Connor. Director: George Fitzmaurice.

1936—"Libeled Lady"

M-G-M. Cast: William Powell, Myrna Loy, Spencer Tracy, Walter Connolly, Charlie Grapewin, Cora Witherspoon, E. E. Clive. Director: Jack Conway.

1937—"Personal Property"

M-G-M. Cast: Robert Taylor, Reginald Owen, Una O'Connor, E. E. Clive, Cora Witherspoon. Director: W. S. Van Dyke.

1937—"Saratoga"

M-G-M. Cast: Clark Gable, Walter Pidgeon, Lionel Barrymore. Director: Jack Conway.

INSERT PICTURE CREDITS

Pictures supplied by CULVER PICTURES
are on pages:
65, 66, 67, 68, 69, 70, 71, 72, 73, 74, 75, 76,
77, 78, 80, 81, 82, 83, 84, 85, 86, 87,
88, 89, 90, 91, 92, 93, 94

Pictures supplied by PENGUIN PHOTO
are on pages:
75, 77, 78, 79, 83, 84, 95, 96